The 100 Greatest Everton moments

This book was first published in 2008 by NSNO via Lulu.com

Copyright © 2008 NSNO.co.uk

The right of the editor, Simon Paul, to be identified as the editor of this book has been asserted to him in accordance with the Copyright, Design and Patents Act 1988. The rights of contributors, Joe Jennings, Chris Lee, Liam Thompson, and Andrew Baker are also covered with this Act.

ISBN 978-1-4092-3178-3

All rights reserved. No part of this publication may be reproduced, stored in a retrieval system, or transmitted, in any other form, or by any other means, electronic, chemical, mechanic, photocopying, recording, or otherwise, without the prior permission of the publisher.

The 100 Greatest Everton Moments

Introduction

In this book we aim to chart what we have chosen as the 100 best moments in Everton history. From the congregation at St Domingo's church deciding to start up a football team to keep their cricket team fit in the winter, to Yakubu scoring the last of his 20 goals in the 2007-08 season, we aim to follow Everton's illustrious history one major step at a time.

We have spoken to a number of former Everton players, and supporters who have been through the thick and thin of being an Evertonian. From Tony Kay feeling proud to come back to Merseyside, to Colin Harvey dreaming about his best Everton goal, to George Orr, who stands outside the Winslow every game selling his fanzine taking a trip down memory lane to reminisce over falling head over heels for the player we call The Golden Vision. These personal "greatest moments" that we are proud to include in this book prove what Alan Ball said to be true: "Once Everton has touched you, nothing will ever be the same again."

There has been something of an upturn in Everton's fortunes in recent years, with the Blues qualifying for European competitions three times from the last four seasons, and the manager breaking the club's transfer record each season, but as we all like to sing "If you know your history"....

Were you at Notts County when Andy Gray dug a trench with his nose as he headed the Blues into the next round of the cup? How about when Bob Latchford scored his 30th goal of the 1977-78 season? Have your parents or grandparents told you of the great days they saw growing up as an Evertonian? This book aims to provide a permanent collection of the greatest moments of Everton's illustrious history. Whether you were there, have heard the story a hundred times before, or finding something new, we hope you enjoy this collection of fantastic Evertonian memories...

Foreword by Dave Prentice

DAVEY SMALLMAN'S acrobatic volley against Sheffield United hasn't made this particular top ton. But that's the beauty of 'Greatest Moment' lists. Everyone has their own special occasions they hold personally dear – and it's great to listen to other people's.

Smallman's razor sharp reactions were the highlight of my first Saturday afternoon visit to Goodison Park (my first match was an Easter Monday and the second a Friday night) which is why it has personal resonance.
But you'll have plenty of others.

We do our fair share of moaning about Everton. But in the last 130 years we've probably been granted more than our fair share of truly 'great' moments.

Here's just a handful of my own: Sharpie's goal at Wembley, Latch's semi-final diving header, Latch's last minute equaliser at Hillsborough, Latch's four goals at Loftus Road - in fact anything to do with Bob Latchford, the sense of pride at seeing Graham Stuart snatch the ball off Neville Southall and demand that Wimbledon penalty, Unsy's penalty kick against Liverpool, Bayern Munich, the final whistle at Wembley in 1995, Highbury '84, Andy Gray's diving headers against Sunderland and Andy King's first against the Reds.

And that's just off the top of my head. Sometimes we focus too much on the negatives and forget how fortunate we've actually been.

Let's face it, you might have been born a Chelsea fan, or Sunderland or God forbid, Newcastle.

So settle back and enjoy some of the greatest moments in Everton's long and illustrious history. And count your blessings . . . all 100 of them.

1. **St Domingo's Church deciding to create a football team in order to keep their cricket team fit during the winter months and choosing Stanley Park as their home pitch in 1878**

The church of St Domingo, which sat at the top of St Domingo Vale and St Domingo Grove in Everton, was just six years old when Rev BS Chambers channelled the sporting ambitions of the boys of the church into a cricket club, and in 1878 the church formed a football club to keep it's cricketers fit during the winter months.

St Domingo's did not play in any organised league – the football league was still a decade away – and instead played in exhibition matches against teams from other parishes. And, although the FA Cup started in 1871, it would be eight years after the club's inception before the first expedition into the competition would be taken.

Football was still a very disorganised pastime, and there were no formal colours worn by St Domingo's, and the formation practised in the early days was a nose-bleed inducing 2-2-6 attacking menace.

2. **The decision to change the name to Everton in 1879**

The footballers of St Domingo's proved to be a popular attraction in Liverpool and within just twelve months the committee were acutely aware that the club was attracting players and spectators from a wider area.

To recognise this fact, and to make the club more accessible to these "outsiders" a decision was taken at The Queen's Head Hotel to change the name to Everton Football Club. Ties between the church and the football club remained strong though, and George Mahon, organist at St Domingo's would later take the club to Goodison Park.

3. Everton's first game, on 20th December 1879, which they won, 6-0.

A month after the boys of St Domingo formally became Everton Football Club, they played their first game with their new name, playing in Blue and White stripes in the South East corner of Stanley Park, and beating St Peters 6-0.

Attendances for games such as these were growing at quite a rate, and early games could attract up to 2,000 people to line the touchlines to watch Everton play.

4. The move to Priory Road in 1882

Everton constructed a small stand and a dressing room at Priory Road, but the first game played there was a disappointment to the club. It was played between a Liverpool representative team and Walsall and yielded gate receipts of just fourteen shillings (which is about 70p today).

The club's first success came on Priory Road when Everton defeated Earlestown in the final of the Liverpool Cup in 1884.

However, Everton's cup win had repercussions for

the club. Mr. Cruitt became fed up of the noise and unruly supporters on his land and told the club to find another ground.

5. Everton's first ever cup win in 1884 - the Liverpool Cup

Everton won their first piece of silverware just six years after the boys from St Domingo started out on their journey to Premier League giants in the shape of the Liverpool Cup, a competition the Blues still find themselves in the final of on a regular basis today – albeit by fielding youth players and reserves.

They defeated local rivals Earlestown to claim the cup which would be won 17 times over the next four decades. Earlestown did, however, get revenge the following year, winning the cup with Everton desperately claiming an equalising goal had been chalked off. Spectators and players alike were certain the ball had gone between the posts, but with the invention of goal nets still seven years away, the referee's (or umpire as they were still called) decision was final.

6. The move to Anfield 3 months later

Just like at Priory Road, Everton did not own Anfield. The land was owned by local brewers, the Orrell brothers, who leased it to the club for an annual donation to Stanley Hospital. However, on arrival at Anfield, the ground had to be prepared.

Everton officials and players, helped by the fans,

took up spades, hammers, nails and barrows and turned what was a pasture on Anfield Road into a football ground.

A certain Mr John Houlding, then Everton's president as well as Lord Mayor of Liverpool, agreed to act as representative tenant for the club on Orrell's land, a relationship that would last eight years.

7. Being founder members of the Football League, and later the Premier League.

Everton, Accrington Stanley, Aston Villa, Blackburn Rovers, Bolton Wanderers, Burnley, Derby County, Notts County, Preston North End, West Brom, and Wolves joined together in 1888 in a bid to regulate football fixtures and formed the football league. Prior to this, football matches could be cancelled at the last minute if a team had been lured into a more lucrative game, and players would switch teams to whoever could offer them a game, or more money. The creation of the Football League would change this, and add formality to the game.

Everton, however, were a surprise inclusion in the League, and were viewed by many members as one of the weaker sides. Local rivals Bootle felt they should have been included in the League, and the exact reasoning behind Everton's inclusion is unknown.

104 years later, Everton were part of the elite that formed the Premier League, a new extension and top-tier of the Football League, originally labelled a "breakaway Super League" but very quickly it became apparent that there was very little difference between the new Premier League and the old First Division – other than financial. Everton finished the first season of the Football League in 6th place, and the Premier League in 13th.

8. The first league game - a 2-1 win over Accrington Stanley

12,000 supporters watched Everton's first ever league game which saw the Toffeemen overcome Accrington Stanley 2-1. The Liverpool Mercury reported that the weather was "fine, with a strong sun and very little wind" and that "the ground was in good order." Aside from the weather report, however, the reporter made very little of a game that would become such a memorable moment in Everton's history.

Fleming was Everton's scorer on the day, September 8th 1888 for those paying attention, which saw the Accrington goalkeeper fracture a rib in making a save from Edgar Chadwick.

Stanley won the return game on December 29th, but Everton went on to have a respectable first season in the newly former League and finished sixth.

9. Everton's record win - an 11-2 thrashing of Derby County in the FA Cup in 1890

The FA Cup was not one of Everton's favourite competitions in the early days of the Toffeemen, but on January 18th 1890, it witnessed the club's greatest win, beating Derby County 11-2 at Anfield.

Three players scored hat-tricks infront of the 9,000 strong crowd; Alec Brady, Frederick Geary, and Alfred Millward, while David Kirkwood scored one of his two Everton goals, and Scottish full-back Daniel Doyle took the opportunity to score his only Everton goal.

The Liverpool Courier's match report claimed that the home side could easily have taken more than the 3-2 lead into the break, and accused Fred Geary of missing more than his fair share of chances! His second and third were Everton's tenth and eleventh, with the latter being scored whilst the player was lying on his back.

Geary also scored in the next round of the Cup, away to Stoke City, but the Potters ran out 4-2 winners and Everton's love affair with the FA Cup was put on hold once again.

10. Sam Chedgzoy dribbling the ball into the net from a corner kick - forcing a change in the rules!

Following a change in the rules in 1923 to allow a goal to be scored directly from a corner, Sam Chedgzoy would force a swift re-wording of the rules a year later. Feigning to take a conventional corner, Chedgzoy took control of the ball and dribbled it into the goal at White Hart Lane on April

12th 1924. The referee disallowed the goal, but later the FA recognised that this approach was perfectly legal – and promptly re-worded Law XVII to state that a corner taker can only play the ball once.

11. Winning our first league title in 1891

Everton first celebrated a Championship title at Anfield, before our modern-day local rivals were even a twinkle in their founders' eyes, a year after finishing second to Preston North End. In 1890 Everton had finished just two points being North End, but had shown signs of the forthcoming success with massive wins against Stoke (8-0) and Aston Villa (7-0).

That success came the following year and in a similar emphatic manner. Once again two points separated the sides, but it was Everton who came out on top, A 7-0 win over Derby County was joined by three 5-0 wins (against Wolves, Bolton and, again, Aston Villa) as Everton showed that they were hoping to become accustomed to the winning feeling.

The Everton fanatics did have to wait for their glory though. First placed Everton played second placed Preston in the penultimate game of the season, and with four points between them, the game would today have been played on a Sunday, at dinnertime, and been given a fancy title. Not in 1891 though, although Preston did follow the script and beat Everton, meaning the title race would go down the last day of the season – which was two months away!

In typical Everton fashion, that last day was full of stress for the 2,000 followers who travelled to Turf Moor to see the side go ahead against Burnley, only to see the lead relinquished. A draw would be enough, but when Everton fell behind, and an equalising chance got stuck in the mud in front of the goal, the final whistle was greeted with groans and a bemused Everton following trudged home unsure of their team's fate. The celebrations got under way soon after the fans had returned home to see the evening papers though – Sunderland had beaten Preston, and the title was Everton's for the first time.

12. The move from Anfield in 1892

In Everton's first 15 years, it must have seemed that winning silverware was a perfect excuse to move – or for landlords to increase the rent, as was the case when John Houlding tried to form a limited company through which Everton would buy land adjacent to Anfield, as well as the ground itself, for over £9,000. At first this deal was accepted, until a certain George Mahon stepped forward to intervene.

Organist at St Domingo's, Mahon had strong links with the "old guard" of Everton and was about to take his place in Everton history as he objected to the proposal to line Houlding's pockets, and a meeting was called to decide where Everton would move to.

Mahon, like many of his successors at Everton, was heckled from the floor when he mentioned moving to a new ground. "Yer can't find one!" shouted one onlooker, to which Mahon calmly responded "I've got one in my pocket." That ground was Mere Green Fields, which would become Goodison Park.

Houlding was ejected from Everton's committee, and after failing in a bid to create a rival team with the name "The Everton Football Club and Athletic Ground Company Limited" he was forced to pay Everton £250 compensation for building the stands at Anfield. Mahon and his supporters had won, and work began on Goodison Park, which would break new ground in football stadia for many years to come.

13. Everton beating Liverpool 3-0 in the first derby in 1894

Starting as they went to go on, the first Everton side to meet one bearing the name "Liverpool Football Club" ran out victorious in the first of the most fiercely contested local "derbies" in the Football League. It was Liverpool's first season in the top flight – although they will want to forget it, as they were relegated while Everton finished runners' up. The first derby at Goodison ended 3-0, with goals from Bell, Latta, and McInnes, while Kelso and Latta scored Everton's goals in their first return visit to Anfield, which ended 2-2.

14. The decision to adopt the famous Royal Blue and White in 1902

Everton were the first team to adopt the Royal Blue that we instantly associate with the club today, but it took 14 years before the colours were finally formalised.

Early Everton teams played in blue and white stripes, followed by salmon pink shirts and blue shorts, but as the club attracted more and more players, and could not afford to provide shirts for each new player, a decision was taken to dye the shirts and shorts black, and sew on a sash of scarlet red! This led early Everton sides to be nicknamed "The Black Watch" and Everton paid tribute to this early kit in 2002-03 when the third kit was pure black shirts and shorts – but without the red!

The kit has seen many changes through the years, but the Royal Blue has remained – albeit in various shades – and quickly became strongly associated with the maritime life on Merseyside, and the Royal Blue Mersey remains a popular terrace chant today.

15. Winning the FA Cup in 1906

It took Everton twenty years to win their first FA Cup, and after an early disinterest in the competition (only joining in fifteen years after it's inception) the Blues finally got 'cup fever' in 1906.

Early cup finals were held at a variety of different venues, with Goodison Park playing host to one in 1894, but Everton's first cup final glory came in the capital, at The Crystal Palace, where 75,000 fans watched the Blues lift the cup.

Everton weren't favourites though. Newcastle had been denied the 'double' a season before, and were hotly tipped to win against Everton – although both sides were at full strength that day, having been fined for fielding weakened sides the week before the final.

The game kicked off at 3:29pm and at five to five, the Blues took the decisive lead through Alex

"Sandy" Young and the cup was on its way to Merseyside for the first time.

16. Keeping the League title for four years during World War One

War had already broken out when Everton kicked off the 1914-15 season with a 3-1 win at White Hart Lane, but with the general consensus in the country being that the war would be over before Christmas, the Football League decided that competition would continue. However, after Christmas public opinion changed, and it was clear that national league football would be put on hold at the end of the season.

Everton ended the league campaign with a draw at Chelsea nine days after a win at Manchester City had put them top of the division for the first time that season. The league title was Everton's, and would remain in the possession of the Blues until football on August 20th, 1919.

17. Signing Dixie Dean

William Ralph "Dixie" Dean was causing quite a stir in the early 1920's at Merseyside's "third" club, Tranmere, scoring five times in a reserve game in his first full season at the age of just 16, and attracting the attentions of every major club of the day – including, naturally, Everton.

Manchester United, Liverpool, Aston Villa and Newcastle all tracked the young Dean, the latter even showing them around St James' Park – he was "unimpressed" – before his beloved Everton came in for him. And at just 18, Dean's transfer to Everton was completed for £3,000 and a glorious period in Everton's history was just about to get under way.

18. Dixie's 60

Three years after signing for Everton, Dixie Dean ensured his name was etched forever into not just Everton history, but global football history, by scoring more goals than anyone else in top flight football would ever muster.

By the last game of the season, Everton were champions, and had scored 99 goals – 57 from Dean – and were entertaining Arsenal in the final game of the season. Dean needed three to get his record, and made quick work of it, scoring his first (and Everton's 100th of the season) after just three minutes. When a second followed soon after from the penalty spot, the fact that Arsenal fought back to 2-2 was secondary to every Evertonian inside Goodison Park.

On 82 minutes, Dean headed his 60th from a corner, and Goodison erupted as only it can. Mischievous commentators at the time said that the cheers were so loud they sent the pigeons sitting on the Pier Head scattering into the sky, and while this may not strictly be true, the cheers did not let up even after Arsenal had once again levelled the game and the final whistle blew. Everton were in Dixieland, much to the bemusement of the man himself, who said of his 60th goal, "I just bowed but the crowd went wild. Somebody ran onto the pitch and stuck his whiskers in my face trying to kiss me!"

19. Employing the first Everton manager

Theo Kelly was Everton's first "official" manager, in the modern sense of the word, after years of resistance from Everton to embrace the new position, and was the first man to take sole responsibility for team selection and transfers in 1939, before this, it had been the responsibility of board members and the club captain.

Kelly had been club secretary and would go on to spend nine years as Everton manager, although the first seven were spent managing the Division One Champions in regional wartime leagues, and when war was over he upset Evertonians by selling Tommy Lawton to Chelsea for £11,000.

Kelly reverted back to his previous role as secretary in 1948 when Cliff Britton returned to the club as manager (he had previously been an FA Cup winning wing-half with the Blues) but Everton had embraced the new age of football and the stage was set for Harry Catterick, Howard Kendall, and David Moyes to follow in Kelly's footsteps.

20. The Dixie Dean Cup Final

"All I want is one more trophy to 'make the set'" said Dixie before the 1933 FA Cup Final, and 'make the set' he did, scoring Everton's second on the way to the Blues' second FA Cup win, and the first at Wembley.

An error from the Manchester City keeper Langford saw a cross from future Everton boss Cliff Britton bundled over the line by Dean using the back of his head, and sending both goalkeeper and striker crashing into the net alongside the ball.

Dean had made history in more ways than one, and April 29th 1933 was no different, becoming the first player to wear the number nine shirt as part of an experiment to help identify players, with Everton wearing 1-11 and City wearing 12-22. The City captain said afterwards, "Dean was an inspiration to his men, and the whole eleven played awfully well."

21. The Number 9 shirt

Evertonians have a longstanding love affair with the number nine shirt. From the days of Dixie Dean, who right through his successor Tommy Lawton, Dave Hickson, Alex Young, Joe Royle, Bob Latchford, Graeme Sharp, and Duncan Ferguson. The number nine shirt at Everton is sacred, and must be earned if strikers want to join those illustrious ranks.

I have been watching Everton for over 50 years, and when I think about my Greatest Everton Moment, surprisingly, it is not difficult to narrow it down. Everton V Tottenham at Goodison Park on 20th April 1963.

67,650 other fans were there to witness the best goal I have ever seen. Alex Young rose into the air hovered and flicked his Golden Head onto the ball; it went as straight as an arrow into the Spurs net. With five games to go this was to be the title clincher as Spurs were the favourites but Everton on that day were magical.

> The Golden Vision was an ever present in what was the worst winter for half a century, the delicate little player with blistered feet became an Everton Legend and is still the best Everton player I have ever seen.
>
> **George Orr** - Editor of the *BlueBlood* fanzine

22. Signing Tommy Lawton

On December 31st 1936, Dixie Dean was sent to Lime Street Station – by tram – to meet the player who was to be his replacement and bring him to Goodison Park. This was no publicity stunt, however, and the modern-day frenzy of media that would follow such an act was completely unheard of in these still innocent days of footballers using public transport, and the two travelled back to Goodison without incident.

Over the next six months Dean monitored his young successor's progress through the reserves, and in the summer told the board that he felt Lawton was ready and just three days before his 18th birthday, Lawton became the youngest player to score in a Merseyside derby, after scoring his first Everton goal in his second appearance a month earlier.

There never had been, and never will be, a greater handover of the number nine shirt at Everton, as one legend who had joined the Blues as a youngster handed over to another who would spend 9 years at the Blues.

Lawton's reign at Everton, however, would be interrupted by war, but he managed to score an amazing 222 goals in 209 first team appearances (including wartime regional league games.

23. Keeping the league for another six years

When the second Great War broke out, unlike twenty five years earlier, football was abandoned almost immediately, and the three games of the 1939-40 season were scratched, meaning that Everton kept the league trophy for a further six years.

Taking the top position on February 4th with a 3-0 win against Liverpool at Anfield, Everton never looked back and were crowned champions well before the final day defeat away to Grimsby.

24. 78,299 fans inside Goodison Park

On September 18th, 1948, more people than ever before – and than will ever be seen again – crammed inside Goodison Park for the Merseyside derby. The year before, more than 66,000 people had watched the corresponding fixture, and that season Goodison had seen over 74,000 for an FA Cup tie between Liverpool and Manchester United. But those figures were blown away when 78,299 supporters took to the stands for this derby.

Attendances all over the country were rising as the UK made hard work of the climb out of post-war struggles, and football provided much needed respite from work and ration books, and this game didn't disappoint.

Future Liverpool manager Joe Fagan put the Kopites ahead after TG Jones had left the pitch for treatment on what was described in the local media as a "mystery injury". Jones was given the chance to remedy his absence when Everton were awarded a penalty (yes, there was a time when Everton got penalties against Liverpool!) but he gave the ball to Scottish centre-forward Ephraim Dodds, whose shot was very nearly saved, but squirmed into the net.

Ted Sagar put in a performance worthy of winning the game for Everton, saving magnificently from Fagan and Billy Liddell, but the game ended 1-1 with Everton rooted to the bottom of Division One, albeit with a huge following.

25. Dave Hickson's FA Cup heroics

In 1953, Dave Hickson forever etched his name into Everton folklore and showed why, when he made the statement "I would have broken any bone in my body for any football club, but I would have died for Everton" that he wasn't simply paying lip-service.

With Everton in the Second Division, their exploits in beating Ipswich and Nottingham Forest were already quite an accomplishment, but they weren't done yet – and as a near record crowd of 78,000 looked on at Goodison Park the Blues put Manchester United to the sword.

United took the lead in the first half, but Hickson and his team were having none of it. Tommy Eglington stole in with an equaliser soon after, and just before half time, Hickson went in bravely with his head where most would have feared put their feet, and emerged with a wound above his right eye. Minutes after, he was back on the pitch, dabbing the gaping wound with his hankie and even heading against the post before being told by the referee to go off and get his wound dressed. Hickson refused, and on the hour mark he fired Everton's winner. With his eye still showing the scars of the United clash, Hickson fired Everton into the semi-finals with the only goal of a 1-0 win against Aston Villa.

Everton lost the semi-final 4-3 against Nat Lofthouse's Bolton Wanderers, with Hickson again requiring 15 minutes treatment on yet another head wound, but the "Cannonball Kid" had proved he was worthy of the Everton number 9 shirt, and wore it 243 times, scoring 111 in the process.

26. Promotion from Division Two

Everton were relegated to the old Second Division in 1951, and spent a painful three seasons out of the top flight before being promoted once again in 1954 as runners up to Leicester City in a close fought race to promotion, aided by Everton's 20 goals in 3 game spell.

The return to Division One came on the back of a six game unbeaten run at the end of the season, culminating with a 4-0 win over Oldham at Boundary Park. Promotion was a relief, and a signal of intent that success was what Everton were after. Little did the likes of Ted Sagar and Dave Hickson realise that they were to put Everton on the road to a spell in the top division of English football that still hasn't ended, and shows no signs of ending soon.

27. Everton 5 Manchester United 2

The 1950's were hard times for Evertonians, and although top flight football was secured in 1954, supporters had little to cheer while Sir John

Moores was involved in buying the club and setting about putting the right people in place to bring the success of the 60's — but there were highlights, and beating Manchester United 5-2 at Old Trafford was one such moment.

George Kirby, cited by Jack Charlton as the hardest man he had ever played against, scored two for Everton who were sitting eighteenth in the league, while Don Donovan added a third, Tommy Eglington a fourth, and Tony McNamara a fifth. Even in our darkest days, Everton could spank The Busby Babes in their second championship season!

28. The adoption of the club crest

In the early days of Everton's existence the club used a number of different images to represent itself graphically — including the Liver Bird, a long time before that other lot across the park decided it would be an iconic image!

In the 1938, however, Theo Kelly registered a new coat of arms for the club to appear on official ties, and decided to use the "beacon" or "tower" that stands on Everton Brow to represent the area of Everton itself. The shape of the badge, however, can also be traced back to an early medal to commemorate a match in 1893 against Newton Heath (who later became Manchester United) in aid of the Life Boat Fund.

The choice of the "tower", known as Prince Rupert's Tower, was a bold move, and one that would prove increasingly popular with supporters, and become an iconic "Everton" image – indeed, it is used as NSNO's own logo! – and although the exact history of the tower is clouded, it has stood since 1787 and has had a number of uses, including a bridewell – where residents of Everton were locked up before attending court.

The badge was used on official paperwork and on club ties, and first appeared on the shirts of Everton players in 1980 with the latin inscription "Nil Satis Nisi Optimum" which means "Nothing Satisfies but the Best."

I've been blessed to have met many of the former players and I cherish all of those memories, but the one incident which really sticks in my mind came at the Adelphi hotel in March 2001.

Gordon Watson had attended the previous Hall of Fame dinner in a wheelchair and was sad that he couldn't get on to the stage, under his own steam, to speak to the fans. He vowed that the next year, he would do just that.

Blueblood, the former players' foundation, paid for him to have a hip replacement that year and I went to his house with the charity's founder, David France, to see how he was recovering. Not only did Gordon open the front door on his own two feet, he showed us his rediscovered agility by performing a series of exercises while regaling us of his memories: leaving Blyth Spartans and travelling to Liverpool on a charabanc as a nervous teenager in 1933, realising the hulk of a man whose shadow filled the dressing-room door was Dixie Dean — 'Hello kid, don't call me Dixie, call me Bill' — and finally making his first-team debut at left-half in January 1937.

The 2001 Hall of Fame dinner was a celebration of Everton's FA Cup winners. Anybody who was lucky enough to attend a bash in those early days will tell

> you how brilliant they were. Z Cars was drowned out by 600 or more delirious Evertonians as dozens of former players filed through to their tables. Then just when we thought the last man had taken his seat, Gordon Watson walked proudly down the aisle holding the FA Cup aloft. It was a magical moment and I swear there wasn't a dry eye in the house. Gordon told me it had been the finest night of his life.
>
> A month later, he passed away and was laid to rest after a touching service at St Luke's Church. He had been a loyal servant of Everton Football Club for nigh on 65 years. He died a happy man.
>
> **Becky Tallentire** – Evertonian author

29. Scoring 20 goals in three games against Derby, Brentford and Plymouth in 1954

In the space of 14 days in February 1954, Everton went on a scoring spree, hitting twenty goals in three games, with fourteen coming in the space of three days!

Derby were hit for six at The Baseball Ground, while in February 24th, Brentford got the same treatment at Goodison Park. Just three days later, Plymouth Argyle conceded eight (although they did score four!) at Goodison to complete a remarkable fortnight as Everton galloped to promotion back to the top flight.

30. Playing Aberdeen four times in America – and not losing

Pre-season tours of America are nothing new to Everton, and although they have seen resurgence under David Moyes and preceded Everton's best seasons in recent history, back in the 1950's the Blues took on a much more punishing schedule stateside for pre-season.

A full month touring the USA in 1956 saw the Blues play 10 fixtures between May 18th and June 17th, including four games against Aberdeen, which ended with an aggregate score of 13-8 to Everton. Other games included a 7-0 win over the American League All Stars and beating Newark Select 4-0.

31. The floodlit derby

On October 9th 1957, Everton lit up the skies around Goodison Park when the first game was played there under floodlights – a 2-0 win over Liverpool infront of 58,000 fans.

Four pylons, each 185 feet high, and housing 36 lamps each, were erected in the corners of the ground and would sway around 3 inches at the top – although those who climbed them claimed it was more like three feet! This would be the fore-runner to many more glorious nights under the lights!

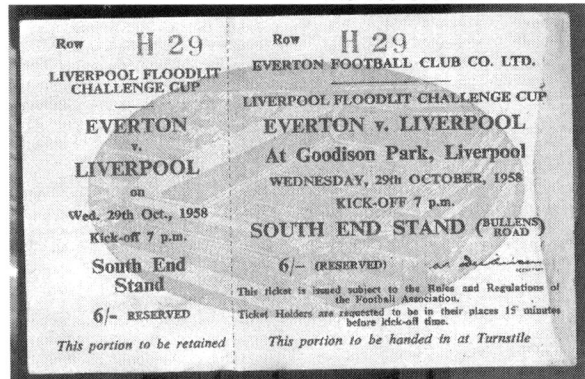

32. Johnny Carey getting sacked in the back of a taxi by Sir John Moores

On April 14th 1961, Everton boss Johnny Carey and his Chairman John Moores went to London for an FA meeting amidst strong speculation that the manager was to be sacked. Demanding clarification, Carey sought a meeting with Moores to find out what was going on, Moores suggested they went to the Grosvenor House Hotel to discuss matters.

Carey persisted in the taxi, and Moores, never one to avoid the issue, got straight to the point and told him he was to be replaced.

It may not have been the most ceremonious way to end his Everton career, but with Carey's sacking came the end of Everton's hard times – the sixties were about to become a golden age for Everton.

It was all such a long time ago that there are only fragments of memories of my short time at Everton. Winning the League in 1963 was a great feeling, but it didn't really come as a surprise to us, we had a brilliant team then, I think Roy Vernon scored a hat-trick that day

Winning my first England cap is right up there. We played Switzerland at the St Jakob stadium and won 8-1. I scored from 30 yards and strangely enough I can remember that quite vividly.

But I think my abiding memory is of the day I went back to Goodison Park for the 100 year celebration in 2002 when we played Tottenham. They had motley bunch of the former players who were to parade on the pitch before the kick off.

I was so nervous waiting in the tunnel and I was last out with Dave Watson. I really didn't know what to expect and the more I thought about it, the worse it was. I realised the Evertonians had every reason to be annoyed with me because I'd cost them £60 000 and they lost out on that money when I was banned for life.

I needn't have worried. I swear the whole stadium stood to applaud me as I made my way round the touch line. People were shouting my name and clambering over the seats to shake my hand. It's giving me goose bumps just thinking about it now. It was truly an amazing moment which I will take with me to my grave.

Tony Kay – Championship winner with Everton in 1963

33. The Golden Vision

As well as being the nickname of one of Everton's great number nine's, "The Golden Vision" is also the name of the a BBC drama-documentary which followed in the footsteps of the likes of Z-Cars and Our Day Out in tracing the movements of a group of scousers doing what scousers do – on this occasion, following football. Religiously!

The film combined a fictional story, in which a pair of star-crossed lovers are determined to rush through their wedding to get to a game at Goodison, with documentary film coverage of Everton in the 1960's.

Unusually for the Everton manager at the time, Harry Catterick, cameras were allowed to film deep inside the inner sanctuary of Bellefield and into training and tactical discussions, and provide a wonderful insight into the workings of Everton Football Club in one of its most successful eras.

First broadcast in 1969, the film strikes a chord with Evertonians in many ways, but perhaps the finest moment is the opening sequence, in which a young girl is interviewed.

What's your name? Jane...

How old are you? Five...

What does your daddy do? Play football...

For who? Everton...

Is he good? Yeah...

What's his name? Alex Young...

34. Harry Catterick taking over as Everton manager

As a player, Harry Catterick had scored 24 goals in 71 appearances for Everton after the Second World War and had even donned the famous number nine shirt between Tommy Lawton and Dave Hickson did so more famously. But it was as manager that he earned the affections of the Everton faithful, and in some style.

He took over as boss in 1961 and had won the league title within two years. Joe Mercer explained, "He put Everton on the map again and played a big part in the development of Bellefield, giving us the facilities to train the players in the best possible way. Harry was a perfectionist."
He paid a record fee of £27,500 for Gordon West from Blackpool, Dennis Stevens, and Johnny Morrissey in his first season, and just before Christmas in 1962 he paid £60,000 for Tony Kay from Sheffield Wednesday. His first championship side was taking shape.

Catterick, backed by Moores, went on to win the FA Cup in 1966, and the League title in 1970 and was the most successful manager of Everton's first 100 year history.

Beating Liverpool is always a great experience, and I've been lucky enough to be on the terraces when we've done it, and on the pitch as a player when we did it too! I remember being on the Gwladys Street with my season ticket in 1978 when Andy King scored for us. We hadn't beaten them for a good few years and then Kingy pops up and sticks it in the top corner. We all went delirious!

Then, four or five years after that, I got to play in the same team as Kingy, and then later on be in a side to beat Liverpool at Anfield for the first time in years too. They're always great days, beating Liverpool!

Derek Mountfield

35. Becoming the Mersey Millionaires

When Sir John Moores took over at Everton Football Club, he was taking charge of the club he had supported as a boy – although he had started out watching Manchester United! He had lived in Eccles as a boy, and his father had taken him to watch United, but when he moved to Liverpool, he started to watch Everton. Having been in the crowd when Dixie Dean scored his 60th goal, Moores had developed a great love of Everton, so in the late 1950's when he was offered the chance to buy into the club, he jumped at it.

At the AGM in 1960, it was announced that Moores had loaned the club £56,000 – interest free – in order to buy new players, after already having funded the purchase of floodlights, and he was elected chairman of the club. The spending had begun.

Moores funded several moves for players under Johnny Carey, but it was his backing of his own man, Harry Catterick, that proved to bring success to Everton. Players such as Alan Ball, Howard Kendall, Tony Kay, and Alex Young, were all bought with Moores' money, and Everton were quickly nicknamed "The Mersey Millionaires", enjoying two league titles and an FA Cup win in just seven years.

36. The '63 Championship

With his side of glittering stars still being assembled, Harry Catterick was under pressure from

John Moores to deliver trophies to Goodison Park, and in 1963, he achieved that goal with the League Championship, proving his new license plate "1 EFC" to be correct!

On the final day of the season Everton needed to beat Fulham to clinch the title, and they did so with consummate ease, pushing the Londoners aside in a 4-1 win to lift the title.

The Blues had won the title in fine form, taking 20 points from the last 24 (10 wins from 12 games) and had shown the world what to expect from Catterick's Everton. Tony Kay and Brian Labone lifted the title in front of 60,000 delirious Evertonians, and afterwards Kay was seen sipping champagne and smoking a 'Winston Churchill' cigar in the Main Stand!

37. Colin Harvey's debut

It was to be the start of a 40 year association with Everton Football Club, but it came as a surprise to a young Colin Harvey, who had assumed his involvement with the first team would be to carry the kit on their visit to the San Siro to face Inter Milan.

The Italian giants stood in the way of Everton and the next round of the European Cup, and for almost three hours it looked as though Everton would get through, aided by 18 year old debutant Harvey.

Harvey was praised for his performance that evening infront of 90,000 spectators at one of the most intimidating atmospheres in the world, but he was back to the reserves the following Saturday to learn his trade before becoming the Everton legend we all know and love.

> It was great the way it all happened, making your debut in the San Siro was just schoolboy stuff, the kind of things you read about in storybooks, but I was back in the reserves the following Saturday for the mini-derby
>
> **Colin Harvey**

38. Gordon West receiving handbags from the Kop

> I thought I would shut them up. Gordon, the miner's son and conker champion from Barnsley, was going to shut the Kop up! So I sauntered along, showed them my bum and then blew some kisses. The following year I got the handbag. It shut me up – and it stayed with me for the rest of my life.
>
> **Gordon West**

Gordon West was an exceptional athlete and an honest professional, who was never afraid of a bit of banter with the players around him, and with the crowd. So much so that his good relationship with Liverpool fans in the Kop saw a tradition grow which saw him presented with a handbag before each derby game by a kopite who would run onto the pitch.

West tells the story of receiving the handbags with a smile in his after-dinner speaking, although he denies any fondness of the Kopites, "They're all ugly bastards" he told guests at an NSNO end of season get together, "Whereas, as you can see in this room, Evertonians are beautiful people!"

39. The World Cup at Goodison Park

Goodison Park is the only club ground in the UK to have played host to a World Cup semi final, and in 1966 it saw the greatest players of the time grace it's lush turf. Pele, Eusebio, and the brave North Korean side all wowed the Goodison crowds, who were treated to the semi final between West Germany and Russia.

Brazil played all of their group games at Goodison, beating Bulgaria 2-0, but losing 3-1 to Portugal and Hungary, as Florian Albert and Eusebio stole the show. Brazil, however, were so impressed by the training facilities they used at Bellefield, that they took ideas back to South America and created their own versions of the training ground.

The game that left it's mark on Goodison during this World Cup, however, was the quarter final between Portugal and North Korea, which ended 5-3 to the Portuguese. The Goodison crowd got behind the Koreans, who had endeared themselves to the Merseyside public during their stay, and the action was spell-binding on the pitch.

40. Eddie Cavanagh's pitch invasion in 1966 at Wembley

Everton had just come back from being 2-0 down at Wembley to Sheffield Wednesday through Mike Trebilcock when, as the players celebrated, one fan took it upon himself to run onto the pitch and celebrate with them.

Eddie Cavannagh, who had played alongside many of the players on the pitch for Everton at youth level, darted onto the pitch in jubilation at

Everton's comeback, and was soon followed by two of London's finest Bobbies. He pranced the length of the Wednesday half, to the amazement of the Everton players, and just as it seemed he had been caught, he shed his jacket and continued his run towards the Everton goal.

Almost on the 18-yard line, he was tackled from behind and brought to the ground, still celebrating as Brian Labone rushed to the scene. Jimmy Harris, wearing the policeman's helmet helped Cavannagh from the pitch, and pleaded with the officers not to throw him out.

Everton went on to win 3-2, and Cavannagh watched the rest from the stands!

41. Re-building the Main Stand

The current stand that sits along Goodison Road – the Main Stand – was the first three tiered stand in the country, and its cantilever roof used groundbreaking technology when it was designed. It replaced a double-decker stand which had stood since 1909 and boasted an enormous terraced area which could hold over 10,000 spectators, as well as an upper seated area and club offices.

The original stand along Goodison Road had been just a cinder bank, but by 1905 it had grown to a huge concrete terrace along its length, supporting a small seating area for the directors and guests of the club, making Goodison the first stadium to include double-deck stands all around the ground.

The redevelopment in 1970 was done whilst play continued infront of crowds at Goodison Park, and with spectators still sitting in parts of the "old" Main Stand while construction went on building the towering structure next to them.

> I think winning the league in 1963, that was a real big one to win, and I was chuffed myself to be an ever-present in the team. Usually you'd get injured and not be able to play, but luckily I avoided injury that season. Winning that was tremendous.
>
> We got huge crowds back then, and the atmosphere was explosive.
>
> **Alex Young**

42. The forming of The Holy Trinity

The trio of Howard Kendall, Colin Harvey, and Alan Ball made up the most famous midfield group in Everton's history – not even the Reid, Bracewell, Steven, and Sheedy could form a more famous midfield formation, despite winning more trophies. But then 'Harvey, Kendall, Ball' rolls off the tongue so much easier and conjures up images of a golden age of English football.

Colin Harvey was the golden boy of the Everton youth system – and would later go on to coach further golden boys after his career as player and manager had ended – and learned his craft through the reserves and tentative expeditions into the first team, and winning the FA Cup before Alan Ball joined him in 1966 – after winning the World Cup.

Ball had been released as a youngster by Wolves because he was 'too small' but was soon showing his doubters what an immense talent he was. Signing for Everton from Blackpool after helping England win the World Cup, Ball was about to prove to be as much of an inspiration for Everton as he was for the national side. Harry Catterick's side now contained two of just eleven men to have won a World Cup for England, and Ball had become Everton's first six-figure player – costing £110,000.

The final piece of the jigsaw was put into place a year later when Howard Kendall was signed from Preston North End for just £80,000. Kendall had been the youngest FA Cup finalist in 1964 and had just 14 months to wait until he was at Wembley again with Everton, again finishing runner up.

The trio wowed the Goodison crowds for a further three years, picking up the league title in 1970 and forming the trio that would continue to be loved and talked about even by generations who never saw them play.

43. Winning the league in 1970

It would have been a travesty if the Everton side that won the title in 1970 had failed to clinch a piece of silverware at all. The bones of the team that won the league in 1963 and 1966 remained, and had been added to in lavish style.

Gordon West, Brian Labone, and Colin Harvey were joined by Kendall, Ball, Royle, Alan Whittle, Johnny Morrissey and John Hurst, and the Blues were tipped to go on to great things. The league title was just a stepping stone, it seemed.

The league was won at Goodison Park, and in a game that was dominated by the Harvey-Kendall-Ball trio who were so influential to Everton for the whole season, infront of a roaring Everton crowd who sent visitors West Brom packing. The fact that the Blues had spent thirty weeks at the top of the league and had only lost once in 1970 - on January 17th - added fuel to the inferno that boiled as the Blues lifted the league for the second time in seven years.

Everton were widely tipped to dominate the 1970's after winning the first Championship of the decade, and the reason they didn't is still subject for many a debate.

44. Winning on penalties in Europe

The thought of penalties sends a shiver down most Everton fan's spines, the thought of penalties in Europe fills most with dread, but it hasn't always been such.

Borussia Monchengladbach were the giants of European football, and in the second round of the European Cup in 1970, came to Goodison Park in search of the scalp of Everton – the English champions – after the Blues had earned a hard-fought 1-1 draw on German soil.

The game ended 1-1 and the teams were plunged into a penalty shoot-out after Johnny Morrissey had put the home side into the lead after just 24 seconds, the visitors equalised on 34 minutes, and the goalkeepers, who had both been excellent during the match were pitted against each other. Andy Rankin, in the Everton goal, came out tops.

Everton led the shoot out with one kick left after Ball, Morrissey, Kendall and Brown had all converted, and Laumann had missed for Borussia. The atmosphere around Goodison was electric, with the noise reaching fever pitch as Muller stepped up for Borussia's last kick. He fired a shot hard to Rankin's right, but the keeper guessed the right way and pushed it around the post. Everton were through to the next round and Rankin was a hero.

45. Duncan McKenzie jumping over a mini

Duncan McKenzie well known as an entertainer, both in his playing days and as an after-dinner speaker, and as a football pundit on local radio, but when he joined Everton he had a reputation for being able to jump over a mini. He had done it at Leeds, in front of 30,000 fans, but his new teammates at Bellefield wanted him to prove he could still do it at Everton. He soon proved he could and he also showed that he could throw a cricket ball the length of a football pitch, and was named as the most famous smoking footballer of the 1970's.

46. Clive Thomas

Clive Thomas' name still rankles with Evertonians after his display in the 1977 FA Cup Semi Final in which Bryan Hamilton's goal was ruled out for "an infringement" by the referee and the Blues were forced into a replay with Liverpool which they lost. He did, however go some way to making amends a year later in third round of the FA Cup against Aston Villa. Everton won 4-1 and Thomas gave what many Villa fans at least claim to have been a very dubious penalty.

Duncan McKenzie, who had been impeded for the penalty, said *"Thomas had an excellent game – a fact which was appreciated by the fans as they gave us all a standing ovation when the final whistle went."*

47. One goal at a time, Bob Latchford

Nobody had scored 30 goals in a league season in either Division One or Division Two for a decade, and in 1977 the Daily Express offered a reward of £10,000 to the player who could make that total in the 1977-78 season. Bob Latchford rose to that challenge in spectacular fashion, although he didn't actually start scoring until the fifth game of the season!

Four goals against QPR, a hat trick against Coventry, and braces against Newcastle, his former club Birmingham, Leicester, Man Utd, and one in each game against Chelsea that season, soon had him on target for the prize. It was, in fact, against Chelsea that he completed the task in "Roy of the Rovers" fashion.

Heading into the game against Chelsea, "The Latch" needed two to claim the prize, in much the same way as Dixie Dean had required three to complete his 60 fifty years earlier. It started so well for Everton, but not for Latchford, with 72 minutes gone, Everton are 3-0 up but Latchford hasn't scored yet! A cross from Mick Buckley, however, was about to change that, as the Latch rose and headed in his 29th of the season. Goodison erupted.

A few minutes later Latchford finds himself in the box again as a ball comes in, only for Mike Lyons to pounce and head home Everton's fifth. The groans echoed around Goodison and Lyons celebrated by muttering a muted "Sorry" to Latchford. He made amends almost immediately though, backing into Chelsea defender Micky Droy and hitting the deck like a sack of spuds – penalty! There was only going to be one taker...

With 13 minutes of the season remaining, Latchford blasted his 30th of the season past Peter Bonetti and sank to his knees infront of the Gwladys Street in celebration.

He met Dixie Dean in the stands after the game, who congratulated him on his achievement, before reminding him "You're still only half as good as I was!"

48. Andy King's derby goal in 1978

"I've not seen a goal like that in a Merseyside derby for years!" exclaimed the commentator moments after Andy King had smashed the ball into the Liverpool net from a Mike Pejic long ball that had been headed on by Martin Dobson. It was the only goal of the game and Everton were victorious. In typical fashion, two Liverpool stalwarts wouldn't take it lightly, and Graeme Souness claimed the shot was mis-hit, while Phil Thompson claimed it took a deflection.

Perhaps as memorable as the goal itself was King being ushered from the pitch with his interviewer from Match of the Day by a policeman before they had chance to finish their interview!

49. Howard Kendall becoming manager

When asked about taking over at Everton for the first time, Kendall is as modest as when asked about any of his exploits in football – "You don't get the chance to manage a great club like Everton unless they are in some kind of trouble," he told NSNO calmly. In reality, Kendall had just won promotion to the old Second Division with Blackburn Rovers in his first year at Ewood Park, and narrowly missed out on promotion to the first the following year – and when asked if he would have left to join Everton had he managed that feat, Kendall needs a long pause before saying yes!

He had been a firm favourite at Goodison as a player, and had taken tales of his experiences away with him when he was cutting his teeth at Birmingham and Stoke as player-coach, several of which made a lasting impression on his apprentice at Stoke – Adrian Heath – who later became Everton's record signing under Kendall.

"Nothing has happened here since 1970," said Kendall when he joined as manager, "and it will take a bit of time to put it right. But we are expected to win trophies and that is what we will do." It took him three years, but 'win trophies' is exactly what he and his Everton side did – becoming the most successful manager in the club's history over a six year period in the 1980's.

50. John Bailey's goal from the half-way line against Luton Town in 1982

Everton's curly-haired, big hat wearing comedian John Bailey may not have been the most glamorous of players during his career. Playing at left-back doesn't lend itself to being a flare player, but with his lightening speed and fearful tackling, Bailey was always a hit with Evertonians, but on December 18th 1982, he showed he could match Pele for skill!

Very few players score from the halfway line. Pele did, David Beckham did, Nayim did so in the Cup Winners' Cup Final, and John Bailey did as Everton beat Luton Town 5-0 at Goodison Park.

> At the time, I think the pressure was on Howard. Although people say "the goal that turned us around," it was an important goal that set us on our way to go to a League Cup Final, which I think was the catalyst, and of all the goals I scored for Everton, it's the goal that people talk about the most because it meant so much to people at the time and there was all the talk of it possibly being Howard's last game. If that were true, then I couldn't have repaid his faith in me any better.
>
> **Adrian Heath**

51. Kevin Brock's back-pass

Referred to by many as the single most important moment of Howard Kendall's career at Everton, Oxford United's Kevin Brock's appalling back-pass is given credit by Evertonians as the moment that saved Kendall's career, and sent Everton on the road to Wembley in 1984.

Oxford were enjoying the label of giant killers when the sides met in the fifth round of the League Cup on January 18th 1984. Howard Kendall, by contrast, was facing a tough time, with back-page headlines claiming he was close to the sack should the Blues go out of the competition to a third division side. Leeds, Newcastle, and Manchester United had all succumbed to the Manor Ground side, Everton had been Chesterfield, West Ham and Coventry.

The giant killing seemed to be set to continue when Bobby McDonald put Oxford ahead and Everton seemed to be heading out of the League Cup, and Kendall out of Goodison. Then, with nine minutes remaining, the unthinkable happened.

Kevin Brock made a slow, sloppy back-pass towards keeper Steve Hardwick and the quick-footed Adrian Heath stole in behind the defence to calmly put Everton back in contention. A week later Everton beat Oxford 4-1 and were on their way towards yet more great moments.

52. Stoke City away

Another game marked out as a "turning point" in Everton's fortunes in the 1980's is the FA Cup tie away at Stoke City on January 6th 1984.

Struggling at the wrong end of the old Division One, a trip to the Victoria Ground proved a welcome distraction for almost 10,000 Evertonians who made the journey, and before the game they proved to be the inspiration for the 2-0 win. On hearing the noise generated by the massive crowd, Howard Kendall opened the changing room windows and said "If you can't do it for them today then you'll never do it for anybody."

Andy Gray, who we talk about next, broke the deadlock with a diving header, and future assistant manager Alan Irvine made it 2-0 with a wicked left foot free-kick made it 2-0. Everton were through to the next round, and on their way into the history books.

53. Andy Gray's diving header at Notts County

Few players epitomised Everton's fighting spirit during the mid-1980's better than striker Andy Gray. Signed after injury had ravaged what many in football believed to be the end of his career, he was rejuvenated at Goodison Park and repaid the faith shown by Howard Kendall in goals and a galvanising spirit. Graeme Sharp commented that Gray would tell the team before the game "We're not losing this one" as they prepared for each match – and he was seldom wrong!

Gray scored many goals with his head, often putting it where less combative would fear to put their feet! Two against Sunderland into the Gwladys Street, and against Bayern Munich spring to mind, but perhaps his most memorable is the goal at Notts County in the FA Cup quarter final.

Ten thousand of Evertonians had travelled to Nottingham on a wet afternoon and, with one fan even braving the high winds to watch from the top of the floodlight tower, Gray's "greatest moment" arrived. Kevin Sheedy whipped in a free kick from the right that went over the top of Graeme Sharp to the back post. Just as the ball was about to hit the ground, Gray dived headlong towards it and headed home – and Everton into the semi-final – with his nose no more than an inch from the floor.

The travelling Everton fans were elated and Howard Kendall joined in the celebrations as the Blues continued to turn a season that seemed destined for failure, to one which was heading for Everton's

54. Trevor Steven's solo goal against Sunderland

As Everton cruised to the 1984-85 Championship, many teams were put to the sword at Goodison Park by three or four goals, and Sunderland were yet another name to add to the list of conquests by the Blues.

Andy Gray had already scored two, with Graeme Sharp adding another as the Blues lead 3-1, but virtuoso winger Trevor Steven was yet to come up with a fourth.

Picking the ball up on the halfway line, Steven powered down the right hand side infront of the Main Stand towards the Sunderland goal. Opting to cut inside rather than make for the byline, Steven tore inwards to the penalty area before unleashing a venomous shot which smashed into the top corner to complete another resounding win for the blues.

55. Graeme Sharp's volley at Anfield

Referred to simply as "that goal" GraemeSharp's thunderbolt into the Anfield Road end as Everton headed towards the league title in 1985.

In the days when thousands of Evertonians would stand on the Kop, and in other stands at Anfield, the song of choice had been "Going down!" as a taunt to the Liverpool faithful, and when Gary Stevens' long ball was controlled with consummate ease by Sharp, he took the ball around Hansen with a touch, and smashed a volley over a sprawling Bruce Grobbelaar and into the history books as the man who gave Everton victory for the first time in six years in the league over their bitter rivals.

The celebrations were ecstatic, with one fan making himself famous, running onto the pitch looking like one of the Proclaimers and dancing around the pitch like a windmill, a sight seen over and over again thanks to the wonder of the internet!

56. Adrian Heath's header against Southampton

Everton's semi-final against Southampton at Highbury in 1984 will never be forgotten by Evertonians, and it could have gone either way, with two world class keepers – Neville Southall and Peter Shilton – in top form throughout the game. But Adrian Heath proved to be the difference between the sides just 3 minutes from the end of extra time.

This was the first FA Cup semi-final to have gone to extra time, and after Peter Reid's free kick had been touched on by Derek Mountfield, Heath headed home and Everton into the final.

Heath cites the goal as one of his favourite moments in an Everton shirt, "Scoring so late on in injury time of extra time with all the Evertonians running onto the pitch, that was a special day knowing that we were going back to Wembley"

57. Everton 2 Watford 0

The sight of Kevin Ratcliffe triumphantly hoisting the FA Cup infront of 50,000 Evertonians at Wembley Stadium in 1984 is one that brings back all kinds of joyous emotions for several generations of Blues.

For those who had lived through the 1960's, a sense that the glory days were returning. For those who had lived through the 1970's, it was the end of a long, hard wait – and the beginning of a wonderful era. And for those growing up in the 1980's, it brought a sense that Everton were going to be at the very top for a very long time.

Everton were favourites, and even before the game Watford Chairman Elton John was in tears, and it only got worse as Everton dominated possession from early on in the game.

Kevin Richardson's cross was cleared as far as Gary Stevens on 37 minutes, and the right back drove the ball towards the area for Graeme Sharp to control and turn to hit an instant shot. It almost looked like he'd scuffed his shot as it bounced into the Watford net off the post. The celebrations were incredible.

Into the second half and once more Everton dominated, with Trevor Steven and Kevin Richardson again having free reign down each flank. Steven was provider this time, as his cross pitched Andy Gray and Watford keeper Tim Sherwood against each other. "Sherwood didn't collect...." goes the famous commentary, and Andy Gray's bravery once again paid dividends as he headed the ball into the net in the split second it would have taken Sherwood to get a second grasp on the ball. Watford complained, and Sherwood sat dejected on the floor as Everton celebrated what was the winning goal. Everton's season had turned around in dramatic fashion, and a wonderful era had begun.

I made saves that I thought were excellent in training, but no-one gives a monkeys about what you do in training do they! It's transferring it onto the pitch, and if you make one or two good saves during the match then it's good.

Take the Tottenham game, we were going for the league, you make a decent save, and it becomes an even better save. Then the one from Imre Viradi I thought was a decent save to be fair, although I thought I made better, but maybe they were in games that didn't really matter.

I tend to remember most of the mistakes and think "Shit, that was embarrassing," but I don't sit down and think of a particular game and think "Yeah, I made a great save there"

Neville Southall

The Times wrote, "Everton's future, so dark in December, is so amazingly bright. Howard Kendall, the youngest manager to triumph in the final, has watched his side emerge so rapidly that, since the turn of the year, they have surpassed even Liverpool for consistent success." They were about to be proven veritable prophets in the following season.

58. Everton 5 Manchester United 0

Fresh from victory in Bratislava, Everton welcomed Manchester United to Goodison Park in good form in October 1984. United were an expensively assembled side and were favourites to rival Liverpool for the title, but their hopes were dashed as Everton ran rampant and demolished any hopes they had of competing in the league.

Kevin Sheedy opened the scoring with a wonderful headed effort, showing the kind of bravery usually associated with Andy Gray, he rose above Kevin Moran and angled a header into the net after five minutes, requiring stitches and a late-substitution to recover from his efforts, but not before he added a second on 23 minutes.

Adrian Heath fired Everton into a 3-0 half time lead, and the Goodison crowd were in full swing as our rivals from down the M52 began to fade away.

It took until the last 10 minutes to get the fourth and fifth goals, however. Gary Stevens broke forward from right-back and took the ball infield before smashing home from 20 yards, and Graeme Sharp added the fifth from an Adrian Heath corner to send United home with "You'll win **** all again, Manchester" ringing in their ears. Everton were on their way to the Championship.

> To be honest, I think just being given the chance to join such a massive club as Everton is my 'greatest Everton moment.'
>
> At my age, I was thinking I was going to go nowhere, because in those days most of the England team were Second Division players because the clubs wouldn't let them go. Once you signed in those days, you signed for life.
>
> I only got the chance to come to Everton for the simple fact that I was 29 years of age and they thought they'd had the best of me, and it was a record fee and there was no chance to say "no, I'm not going anywhere!"
>
> I actually had a chance to sign for Everton when I was a kid after being involved in a trial at Huddersfield, but I wanted to stay loyal to Huddersfield, I think I must have been stupid!
>
> **Ray Wilson – World Cup Winner**

FOOTBALL ASSOCIATION CHALLENGE CUP COMPETITION

CUP FINAL

SATURDAY 19 MAY
1984
KICK-OFF 3.00p.m.

E·V·E·R·T·O·N
▼
W·A·T·F·O·R·D

Wembley Stadium

OFFICIAL SOUVENIR
PROGRAMME 80p

59. Bayern Munich

Bayern Munich were the best side on mainland Europe in the mid-1980's, and when Everton went to the Olympic Stadium in Munich, and returned with a priceless draw, the return visit brought high expectations and a mass hysteria not seen since the Beatles were in town.

On Wednesday, 24th April 1985, many more than the 49,000 "official" attendance crowd packed into Goodison Park – and on top of St Luke's Church – to watch Everton take on the German maestros on our own patch.

Everton dominated from the start, but somehow found themselves a goal down at half time – they were giving one of Europe's finest sides a head start! This didn't deter the Goodison faithful, and the noise inspired Howard Kendall to tell his team to carry on as they were doing, and that "the Gwladys Street will suck the ball in."

It did, but not without the help of their Everton heroes on the pitch. A long throw from the right by Gary Stevens was flicked on by Andy Gray – who dominated the air against the Germans – for Graeme Sharp to nod home and Everton were level.

Everton's second came after another long throw from the right-back but this time it was Sharp's turn to cause chaos for the Bayern defence and the ball was flicked to Andy Gray to tap into an empty net as Jean Marie Pfaff stood with his hand up, seemingly complaining of a foul, although replays show that he was actually impeded by his own defender – and that a goalkeeper should never be on that side of his goalpost!

Everton were ahead, and Goodison was electric, but it wasn't finished there. Trevor Steven had had an indifferent game, but it was he who finished Bayern off. Paul Bracewell played the ball forward to Gray who, without even looking up, played the ball straight into Steven's path for the midfielder to sprint forward in space. His finish was clinical, and as he wheeled away in delight the ball nestled into the bottom left corner of the Gwladys Street goal. Mission accomplished. Rotterdam here we come!

After the game, German coach Uli Hoeness shouted at Andy Gray as he walked off the pitch "That was not football, you are all crazy men!" More mainstream publications have quoted Andy Gray as replying with "No, we are winners!" but many will tell you that the actual reply – from most of the Everton players and staff – was a simple "Fuck off!"

60. Champions in 1985

The 1985 Championship was won with five games to spare and with two Cup Finals to look forward to as the Blues beat Queens Park Rangers on May 5th 1985 at Goodison Park courtesy of goals from Graeme Sharp and Derek Mountfield. It was a real party atmosphere inside Goodison Park, with newly crowned "Player of the Year" Neville Southall cheered onto the pitch before manager Howard Kendall picked up the "Manager of the Month" award, which would soon be followed by the "Manager of the Year" prize.

The Championship had been won in style, typical of the Everton side's way of playing and the trophies that were collected were earned by skilful play and gritty determination. The Blues played over 60 games that season, highlighted in the league with the 5-4 win away at Watford, the 5-0 demolition of Manchester United at home, and the two 1-0 wins over Liverpool.

Everton's first title in 15 years prompted elation from Evertonians, and Sir John Moores said "I never thought I'd live to see another League Championship come to Goodison. It's great to feel free of the domination of Liverpool." And so it was!

61. Rotterdam 1985

For some players involved, there was a sense that they had already played their final, as beating Bayern Munich in the semi-final meant they had beaten the best side in the competition – Everton aside, of course. But for the fans, the occasion was enormous – Everton were in a European final. At last!

Tens of thousands of Evertonians flocked to Rotterdam to watch their heroes lift the European Cup Winners' Cup that day, including one who decided – for a laugh – to see if he could get in for free, climbed the walls of the stadium and sat in his seat, proudly showing off his match ticket intact and unused!

The atmosphere inside the stadium was electric, and Everton were dominant, both on and off the pitch – you would have been forgiven for thinking it was an Everton home game, such little noise came from the Austrian supporters! They had little reason to celebrate however, as a rampaging Everton side set about their task of destroying Rapid Vienna.

It took the Blues almost an hour to break the deadlock though, but when Graeme Sharp pounced on a sloppy backpass he pulled it back into the area for Andy Gray to volley the Blues ahead.

Everton's lead was doubled when Kevin Sheedy and Trevor Steven combined it was from a right-sided corner from the Irishman that went right across the Vienna penalty area for Steven to smash Everton into a two goal lead. Everywhere you looked, blue flags waved and Everton were on their way.

Hans Krankl rounded Neville Southall to pull one back for Vienna, but nobody really believed they would come back into it, and just a minute later Kevin Sheedy burst through the Vienna defence to smash Everton 3-1 ahead, and ensure that Everton's first European trophy was sealed. Goodnight Vienna!

62. Kevin Sheedy "saluting" the Kop after scoring

Kevin Sheedy may have signed from Liverpool, but if any reds had dreamed of him having any kind of affection for his former team, they were soon destroyed when he fired Everton into a lead with a trademark free kick into the Kop End in 1987.

The free kick was perfect. Taken from 25 yards out, to the right of the Liverpool penalty area, Sheedy smashed it into the top left corner of the goal past a despairing keeper and to the joy of Evertonians.

Sheedy said afterwards, "I usually just put one finger up signaling a goal, but, it being the kop end, two fingers automatically went up. I got hauled up in front of the FA and I was like Ted Rogers trying to go from two fingers to one and trying to convince them it wasn't a v-sign."

63. Gary Lineker's first Everton goal

Gary Lineker was signed from Leicester City a year after being instrumental in the Midland's side's promotion to the old Division One, and although a move from Filbert Street had been inevitable, the move was fraught with difficulties. Everton valued him at £400,000, Leicester at £1.25m. Everton were eventually told to pay £800,000 by an independent tribunal.

Lineker's arrival, however, signalled the end of the Everton career of an old favourite – Andy Gray and when 'Links' failed to find the net in his first three games, it seemed he would never win the confidence of the Everton support...

After a disappointing return to his former club Leicester and at home to Coventry and West Brom, Lineker finally got off the mark at Spurs – where he would later play – with the only goal as Everton won 1-0. The following week he scored a hat trick at home against Birmingham City, and followed it with a brace in the 5-1 demolition of Sheffield Wednesday.

By the end of December he had scored 21 goals, prompting Howard Kendall to make the following statement in his programme notes : "This is an exceptional scoring record, and I felt I had to come out and say so after hearing so much criticism of our decision to buy him...I was very pleased when the crowd rose to him on Boxing Day.[a home win against Manchester United in which Lineker scored]"

64. Neville Southall's breathtaking save from Mark Falco at White Hart Lane in 1985

Neville Southall is a big man. Six feet one inches tall and weighing in at fourteen stone when he's not had his tea. For a man of his size to possess the agility that he did was a marvel, and little wonder that he was thought of as the best goalkeeper in the world for much of the mid to late 1980's – and beyond in some circles.

There were many examples of his excellence, but the night he managed to change direction in mid-flight at White Hart Lane will remain at the top of many people's lists of great saves from the big man.

Three minutes from time, Mark Falco bulleted a header goalwards as Spurs tried to equalise Everton's 2-1 advantage. To everyone around it seemed it was going in, but Southall somehow twisted his body in mid-air to get his fingertips to the ball and push it over in a display of lightening reactions and super-human agility.

65. Gary Lineker's goal at Wembley

Wembley was Everton's second home in the 1980's, and in the first FA Cup Final between Everton and Liverpool the famous stadium saw fans of opposing sides standing side by side for the first time in it's history on such a big occasion. The atmosphere was electric and after Everton had seen their rivals steal the league from them on the last day – despite a 6-1 thrashing of Southampton – the stage was set for a cup final like no other.

On 28 minutes, Kenny Dalglish gave away possession in midfield and Peter Reid threaded a wonderful ball through the Liverpool defence for Lineker to chase. He shrugged away from Alan Hansen and raced onto the ball, goalkeeper Bruce

Grobelaar raced out to meet him, and saved Lineker's shot.

The striker, however, was as quick of mind as he was on his feet, and smashed the rebound past the stranded keeper. Everton were ahead and the Blue half of Wembley lit up.

66. Derek Mountfield's celebrations

Derek Mountfield was living the dream. As a boyhood Evertonian he dreamt of lifting the FA Cup for his team, and after signing from Tranmere in 1982, the 1984-85 campaign gave him that chance.

In the semi-final against Luton Town at Villa Park, he scored a late goal to put Everton into another Wembley final. His celebrations were sheer ecstasy, as he wheeled away with his arms straight above his head and his fingers spread as wide as possible, his smile as wide as the Mersey tunnel!

67. Selling Gary Lineker and still winning the league

Just twelve months before selling Gary Lineker, his purchase was seen as a massive error by Everton fans. However, in those twelve months, he had proved himself to be a huge asset to the Everton side he played in, so when the decision was made to sell him to Barcelona for a then record fee, it was criticised by many Evertonians. But they needn't have worried.

Many who played for Everton in those mid-1980's heydays felt that Lineker's signing changed the way they played the game – everything went long to utilise Lineker's pace. In the season before, a handful of players had got into double figures in the scoring charts – with Lineker in the team, Everton still scored goals by the bucketload, but they all came from him. In the 1986-87 season, that changed again, and goals came from all areas of the field – from 16 different players to be precise.

Everton finished the 1986-87 season with 86 points, the same number that had seen them finish second the previous season, but this time, superhuman efforts were enough to clinch the title for the second time in three years.

Forced to play as a squad rather than as a team (Kendall often comments that the 1984-85 side "picked itself") Everton used no fewer than 23 players during this championship winning season which saw Kevin Ratcliffe as the only ever-present in the side.

The title was clinched at Norwich City's Carrow Road, courtesy of a rare Pat Van den Hauwe goal, smashed in from just infront of the penalty spot, and was paraded at Goodison the following week after a 3-1 win over Luton Town.

68. Signing Dave Watson

Howard Kendall had decided he wasn't going to spend too much of the money generated from the Gary Lineker sale, but with Derek Mountfield's injury problems becoming apparent, he needed a partner in the middle of defence for Kevin Ratcliffe. Enter, for £950,000, one Dave Watson, from Norwich.

Watson would go on to play almost 500 times for Everton, and lift the FA Cup in 1995 after becoming a consistent and reliable linchpin of the Everton side – it took a while to earn that role, however.

In his first season he was inconsistent, and a large number among the Everton support were not happy that he was favoured to Derek Mountfield at the heart of the Everton defence. He appeared clumsy and was found out of position on a number of occasions, and was hardly showing the sort of form that you would expect of a player who had already earned his first England cap.

After being dropped early in the 1986-87 season for Derek Mountfield, Watson fought his way back into the side and never looked back. His form returned, and the love affair with the fans began. It would continue for a further twelve years as "Waggy" settled at Everton.

69. Tony Cottee's hat-trick on his debut

Tony Cottee joined Everton and broke the transfer record in a £2.3m move from West Ham, spurning the advances of Arsenal to become Everton's number 10.

He was a goalscorer with a proven pedigree and had already won his first England cap, and when he scored a sensational hat trick in his first game in a Blue shirt, it seemed he would be the answer to Everton's prayers.

He went on to top the goalscoring charts at Everton five seasons out of six, scoring a total of 99 goals for the Blues, but there will always be a feeling that Cottee never lived up to his early promise. When NSNO met Cottee in 2006, he told us he was devastated not to have played alongside

Duncan Ferguson, and when asked if Mike Walker was as shit as we all thought he was, his reply was a candid "He wasn't even *that* good!"

Having been only three years old when the Bayern Munich match took place, stranded in Newcastle for the 4-4 derby and grounded for Joe Royle's first game in charge, I didn't have many options until Wednesday 20 April 2005 came along.

Working for the club was an honour and a privilege – and I suppose that's why this game stands out that little bit more for me. On that evening it was my responsibility to write the minute-by-minute report for the club's website.

Looking back though, I didn't do much for the final ten minutes as I was too busy praying we'd hang on!

When Duncan scored, I'd never heard Goodison so loud. The scenes at the final whistle were incredible and, as I was interviewing the players in the tunnel, a full 20 minutes after the game finished, you could still hear the fans singing inside the ground.

Brian Labone was in reception as I was about to head home. "Fourth place is ours son," he said, patting me on the back. "We'll finish above the other lot now, don't you worry about that."

How could I? I knew he was right – and in our hearts, we all did too.

Martin O'Boyle – author of Bob Latchford's "30"

70. Gwladys Street's last stand

On May 4th 1991, the Gwladys Street waved goodbye to standing at Goodison Park and became part of an all-seater Goodison Park. The last crowd to stand on the Gwladys Street saw the Blues beat Luton Town 1-0, with Tony Cottee rounding the Luton keeper to slot home his 23rd of the season, but the result was of secondary importance to many on the Street End that day.

Never again would you feel the sway of the crowd in full song, or the surge forward in response to a goal, or the uncontrollable "swept up in it all" feeling when you first realise there is simply no point in fighting the momentum caused by 10,000 bodies. Standing at the Street End – or sitting on one of the barriers as many younger lads chose to – was an unforgettable experience, and although key games often lend themselves to the Street once again taking to their feet for the whole game, true standing on the Gwladys Street is now part of Everton folklore.

71. "You never walked alone" banners at the 0-0 derby after Hillsbrough

Hillsbrough was a disaster that rocked football, and but for the toss of a coin, instead of our rivals from across the park mourning supporters, it could easily have been Everton fans that perished in Yorkshire that day.

Merseyside united in support of Liverpool, and for weeks after the tragedy, Evertonians joined their Liverpool supporting friends and family in laying messages of support at Anfield, and at the following Merseyside derby, banners of support and of thanks were shown during an impeccably observed silence for those lost.

The result of the game became secondary, and a goal-less draw could almost have been scripted as fans of both sides stood together for what would be one of the last times before top-flight stadia became became all-seater affairs.

72. The derby to end all derbies

The magic of the FA Cup is something Evertonians can undoubtedly relate to - in this game, that indescribable magic was well and truly alive.

The visitors - arch rivals Liverpool - found themselves firm favourites entering the tie, but Everton were to be undeterred. It was the Toffees' never say die attitude - combined with the sprinkling of quality that remained within the squad - along with some zealous support, that ensured Everton made the ultimate comeback and somehow dragged themselves back into an irretrievable encounter.

The game itself went backwards and forwards - swung side to side - with one side in the ascendancy, then the other. Beardsley had netted two for the Reds, along with Rush and Barnes. Everton found themselves 2-4 down with just over ten minutes remaining.

On came Tony Cottee in extra time to somehow salvage Everton's cup dream - and so he did. Netting two goals, the second in the 114th minute to keep the dream alive, Martin Tyler, as he does, got very excited. Widely considered as the most exciting Merseyside Derby of all time, Everton returning from the dead on four occasions is something Evertonians will never forget. We even won the replay.

73. Accepting Peter Beardsley

When a player has played for Liverpool, and then comes to Everton, they have to be something pretty special to win the affections of Evertonians. Kevin Sheedy had managed it, Alan Harper – despite the nickname "Ugly" from the Gwladys Street – had also found a place in our hearts, Dave Watson was busy with his etching knife, but none of them had been what could be described as "Kop favourites." Peter Beardsley, on the other hand, had been. He was going to have to put in double shifts and hope his natural ability could shine through.

Fortunately, for us all, he worked extra hard, and his ability on the ball was a welcome tonic at Everton from the instant he pulled on the Royal Blue on August 17th 1991.

It was a little over a month later, though, that it became clear that he didn't care what colour shirt he wore – so long as he gave everything for the honour of doing so – in a 3-0 thrashing of Coventry City.

Beardsley had signed for just £1m after Everton had lost out to the Kopites on the signature of Dean Saunders, but it was obvious during this win that fate had dealt manager Howard Kendall a very kind hand as the Geordie finished the season on 20 goals – far superior to that of the Welshman Everton had "lost out" on.

In the game against Coventry, Beardsley scored his first Everton hat-trick, although his first would probably be chalked down to luck rather than skill. David Borrows' attempted clearance smashed against Bearsley's shins and rebounded into the Coventry net. The second was all down to skill and ability, however.

A half-cleared cross fell to the outside of the box and Beardsley smashed it home for the second, while the third came from the penalty spot to spark chants of "One Peter Beardsley" around Goodison Park.

74. Founder members of the Premier League

One hundred and fourteen years after helping found the Football League, Everton were once again at the forefront of the English game in 1992.

The league envisaged a new era of football, with new higher standards for stadia, pitches, and all kinds of other things, but in reality changed the name from Division One and took the leadership away from The Football League, enabling more games to be televised and more money to flood through football's turnstiles.

Everton, however, can be proud of being at the top of the game when such important changes were taking place, and taking advantage of their position.

75. Last day escape against Wimbledon in 1994

Hobbling and frantic from two self-inflicted gashes, Everton rejuvenated to give their gutsiest performance of many a season - of all time maybe - and so remain in the Premier League.. Two goals and one saved (missed by the referee) from Stuart supplied the means by which Everton overcame a two-goal Wimbledon advantage and so leapt through the escape hatch to safety.

Stuart had duly converted the penalty to offer some much needed hope, and a roar unleashing all the relief and fury pent up by Everton's plight engulfed Goodison Park.

The atmosphere was combustible, almost as inflamed as the Wimbledon team bus which had caught fire in dubious circumstances in the early hours preceding the game outside the team's headquarters in Runcorn.

Everton, attacking with menace and penetration found joy through the most unlikely of sources - Barry Horne. This was the moment when hope sprang eternal as Horne let fly from all of 30 yards in our day of destiny. The Gwladys Street stand - who had the best view in the house - watched on as the ball swerved wickedly before cannoning off the post and rustling into the net. Unbelievable elation overcome the Old Lady.

The Toffees - now like hungry wolves - pressed on vehemently and it was to scenes bordering on hallucination that Stuart planted the winning goal into the back of the net. Fans flooded on to the field and fell to their knees in thanks that Everton's 40 years in top-flight football had not come to an discomfiting end, it had been remarkably preserved.

One of the greatest comebacks of all time. We had done it, by hook or by crook - the Everton way.

76. Winning the FA Cup in 1995

Everton had survived the scare of relegation - with new manager Joe Royle steering the club away from the dreaded drop – and had gone on a magical FA Cup run that was to end in glory.

Manchester United were wounded - having lost their league title on the final day to Blackburn Rovers - this was a game they had to win, defeat was unthinkable. But Everton entered the game strain free, we had won our battle and although everyone hoped and believed we could bring home the cup, it simply wasn't deemed feasible nor realistic by anyone outside of Merseyside.

But when has the magic of the FA Cup ever been a rational notion? A resolute and tenacious Everton midfield, combined with a rock solid back four and the evergreen Neville Southall meant the Red Devils were left frustrated, fruitless and trophy-less come the final whistle.

The Blues scored the elusive goal on the half hour mark with Rideout heading home following brilliant work from Messrs Limpar, Jackson and Stuart (who should have scored!) who saw his shot cannon off the bar.

It was a case of clinging on to glory - and so we did. United pounded Everton with everything but the kitchen sink, but it was to no avail. David Unsworth was a man-mountain and Southall produced an amazing double save in the dieing embers, whilst Joe Parkinson showed Paul Ince who really was "The Guvnor." The final whistle blew - Evertonians everywhere embraced -we had done it, the cup was coming home.

77. Last Day escape against Coventry in 1998

This was a game that I had decided not to go to as I couldn't see us getting out of this one especially the way we had succumbed so easily to Arsenal the week before. However the day of the game i woke up and knew i needed to be there. The main problem was I didn't have a ticket and the game was a sell out. At the time i was a 1st year student at JMU living in the Halls of Residence next to the Anglican Cathedral in town and I persuaded one of my house mates to come up to the ground with me to see if we cold get our hands on a couple of tickets.

When i got up to Goodison around 1pm remember there was a muted atmosphere around the stadium and not the usual optimism you normally see on a match day. I managed to get 2 tickets for the main stand from a nice man selling them outside the Wimslow for only £5 above the face value which considering the magnitude of the game was a bargain.

Once in the ground though the atmosphere was electric but tense. The game kicked off at a frantic pace and it took Gareth Farrely only 7 minutes to give Everton the lead. The stadium erupted as if it was letting out all the tension that was still being held in since the Highbury Game. Everton dominated the rest of the half without creating anyting of note.

As we needed to get a better result than Bolton who were playing away at Chelsea there were several people in the stadium listening to that game at the same time and every so often you would get word of what was happening in London from someone in the vicinity. At one point there was an almighty roar from the Park End as they thought Chelsea had taken the lead against the

Trotters and this was followed by celebrations around the rest of the stadium, but it turned out to be a false dawn

> I went to bed that night, knowing my team, and woke up with a different one! Gareth Farrelly wasn't in the side that I'd picked the night before, so someone up there must like me to change my mind. And I thought he was due for one, he'd been ballooning them all over the ground in his attempts to score, but he certainly hit the target that day.
>
> **Howard Kendall**

At half time with the score in London 0-0 the word was that Bolton had started the brighter team and were well on top against a Chelsea side who were playing VfB Stuttgart in the European Cup Winners Cup Final 3 days later.

In the second half Coventry started to come into the game more however news came up from London that Gianluca Vialli has put Chelsea ahead. The stadium again erupted and one of the lasting memories for me of that day is the Everton Fans chanting "Vialli, Vialli".

Nick Barmby's penalty miss with five minutes to go followed by an equaliser from Dion Dublin meant that the last few minutes were nerve racking and the Goodison roar was replaced by a chorus of nervous whistles that is until Chelsea scored again. The referee blew up for full time and 40,000 Evertonians flooded onto the pitch including myself to get their bit of souvenir Goodison turf.

78. Amo's goals against Spurs on the way to Wembley in 1995

Often high deficit score lines tend to flatter the victorious side, but definitely not on this occasion. Everton destroyed Tottenham, and cemented a place in the 1995 FA Cup Final, rooted with unstinting endeavour and precise finishing, with Daniel Amokachi netting two in a comic strip cameo.

Paul Rideout had limped to the sideline with 67 minutes gone, unbeknown his unfortunate injury, and subsequent substitution would cement his Nigerian replacement's name into Goodison folklore.

Everton were just so committed in the pursuit of success, they were to be undeterred. Southall then made an incredible save on 81 minutes, denying Nethercott with his legs. What should have been 2-2 promptly became 3-1 as Southall's hoof ensured the Toffees were on their way to Wembley. Limpar and Horne combined with the latter lifting a splendid cross into the box for 'Amo' to nod home and send the Evertonians behind the goal wild - it was ours, we were there.

The mass elation on three sides of the ground - officially this was branded a neutral venue, but in truth it was home advantage for the Blues - heightened as Limpar combined this time with Ablett for Amokachi to slam home his second and Everton's fourth. The now legendary trademark bop of the head fuelled the Evertonians' love of their energetic African - just rewards for the years of decay.

Blue hearts pounding everywhere, Everton headed for the place they consider their second home - Wembley. Tell me Ma me Ma....

79. 'The Kanchelskis derby'

Acrimonious arrivals are usually undesirable to Evertonians - but with Andrei Kanchelskis it was different, very different. A shoulder injury had prevented the winger from proving his worth, with the agitated supporters desperate to see their £5 million pound man deliver....and deliver he did.

His time to cement a place in the affections of the Everton faithful had finally arrived. Kanchelskis, so triumphant in derby clashes when wearing United red, put the Everton fans into blue heaven when he created and finished the opener in the Anfield Merseyside Derby. The Evertonian contingent was sent into raptures, and rightly so.

The new found hero broke from deep before spreading wide to Paul Rideout on the right flank. Phil Babb as expected, stood off as Rideout shaped to cross, and that allowed time for Kanchelskis to steal into the box and thunder a 12-yard header in off David James' left-hand post - cue delight.

He was not done yet. Limpar found Kanchelskis on the right hand side - with the omnipotent Babb out of position once again - enabling Andrei to strike low and hard, James could only help the ball on its way. Game over, Royle's hoodoo over Evans looked set to continue.

Continue it did. Fowler managed a late consolation, but it wasn't enough - Everton had ruthlessly disposed of their arch rivals. Andrei-mania had well and truly arrived.

80. Duncan Ferguson's first game back after coming back from Newcastle

It was the homecoming of homecomings. The Everton legend that was Duncan Ferguson was well and truly back- and with a bang.

Everton had been outfought, outclassed and totally outran by newly promoted Charlton Athletic, who dominated proceedings despite having only ten men. Everton had taken the lead through "Fox in the Box" Francis Jeffers but Charlton were on top and looking most likely.

On came Ferguson, who had been sold behind manager Walter Smith's back two years previously to secure all three points for the Toffees. Gravesen turned sharply and slipped in Ferguson who drilled in a crisp right foot effort into the bottom right hand corner of the Gwladys Street net, cue bedlam. The Street End exploded into a frenzy of elation, the hero had returned.

Clearly buoyed, Everton sensed more goals - their wish was granted. Jeffers slid in Ferguson who struck with his preferred left foot this time, the ball subsequently looped over the hapless Kiely and the Scot celebrated a brace upon his return "home", the Gwladys Street end crescendo reached climax once more.

It was a fitting end to a night that was always likely to transpire into the Duncan Ferguson show. Through times of despair, Everton needed a hero, Ferguson certainly fitted the criteria.

81. Kevin Campbell's 9 goals in 7 starts on loan in 1998-1999.

Kevin Campbell was as important to Everton's Premier League survival in 1999 as Barry Horne had been four years earlier, and Gareth Farrelly a year before Campbell arrived, and many state that his arrival kept Everton in the Premiership.

If Kevin Campbell scored, Everton won. Braces against Coventry, Newcastle and Charlton gave Everton three crucial wins late in the season, and his crowning glory – a hat-trick against West Ham during a 6-0 drubbing at Goodison – earned him hero worship among Evertonians, and a long contract with the club.

"Super Kev" went on to make over 150 appearances for the Blues and scored almost a goal every three games, often playing through injury and pain to show his commitment to the Blue cause. He also holds the record for number of Premier League goals scored by an un-capped Englishman!

82. Signing Paul Gascoigne.

Gazza was once the darling of English football, and even six years after his exploits in the Euro '96 finals, signing Paul Gascoigne meant bringing a major talent to the club.

Forgetting his personal problems, and his £12,000 a week, Gazza's name in an Everton shirt excited people. He rarely filled 90 minutes with glory, but his touches were awesome and his goal against Bolton summed up what Paul Gascoigne could do for Everton.

He left after his personal problems could no longer be tolerated, but Paul Gascoigne's last great performances in English football came in an Everton shirt.

83. David Moyes' and "The People's Club"

When David Moyes joined Everton, the club, and fans, were in desperate need of a lift – something to kick-start some optimism. The new manager gave us that by uttering just three words – "The People's Club" – and instantly claimed the hearts of the blue half of Merseyside by sending a thunderbolt out to those at Anfield.

> *"I am from a city that is not unlike Liverpool. I am joining the people's football club. The majority of the people you meet on the street are Everton fans."*
>
> **David Moyes**

84. Unsworth welcoming Moyes with a 27 second goal

David Moyes' first game was against Fulham, and he was welcomed to the Goodison turf to huge applause. All he needed now was a win to get the momentum really going. David Unsworth duly delivered the kind of start we could all only have dreamed of, smashing home on 27 seconds to get Moyes' Everton career off to a winning start. Unsworth ran the length of the Fulham half to celebrate with his new manager infront of the dugouts.

85. 100 former players on the pitch

To celebrate being the first club to reach 100 years of top flight football, Everton paraded 100 of our former heroes around Goodison Park during the first home game of the 2002-03 season. Legends such as Gordon West, Brian Labone, Alan Ball, Howard Kendall, and even Tony Kay were greeted by 40,000 Evertonians as the Blues continued to make history.

86. Wayne Rooney's first goal for Everton

"Remember the name" exclaimed the commentator as Wayne Rooney tore away towards the Park End, his teammates giving chase, after he became the Premier League's – and Everton's – youngest goalscorer after beating Arsenal's David Seaman from 30 yards. His control had been instant from a hopeful Thomas Gravesen ball foward, and he turned to see the Gunners defence back off. He looked up, and curled a wicked shot over David Seaman to fire the Blues into a 2-1 lead which would end Arsenal's 42 game unbeaten run.

To say the atmosphere inside Goodison was electric would be an understatement, as people rushed back up the stairs to witness the new Everton hero celebrate his arrival on the Premiership scene.

87. Still being the longest-serving top-flight club

Barring an horrendous run of poor form, Everton will currently still be the longest serving top-flight team. 106 years. The nearest rival, Aston Villa, have yet to reach 100 years in the top flight. The kopites? They're not even close!

88. Rooney's goal against Leeds United

"Do you think Evertonians have found a new hero?" asked the commentary team after Wayne Rooney scored the game's only goal to beat Leeds United at Elland Road for the first time in 51 years.

This was Rooney's second goal for Everton, and what a special one it was. He left a Leeds defender on his backside as he skimmed across the Elland Road turf and fired into the net after collecting the ball from Tony Hibbert. What followed next was scenes of pure elation.

Rooney rushed towards the crowd, and the crowd rushed forwards. The young striker leapt into the air and press photographers captured a moment of Evertonianism at its best as Rooney and his teammates were engulfed in a sea of smiling faces.

89. Lee Carsley's goal against Liverpool

The 2004-05 season saw a new galvanised Everton side in the wake of the departure of Wayne Rooney, and a return to form of a forgotten Walter Smith signing, Lee Carsley.

David Moyes had adopted the 4-5-1 formation and Lee Carsley thrived in the holding midfield role, protecting his defence and feeding the midfielders ahead of him, and even finding himself in advanced positions from time to time, and the defining moment of his season came against Liverpool at Goodison Park.

Everton battled and out-fought Liverpool, with Tim Cahill, Tony Hibbert, and Carsley himself winning their own personal battles on the pitch, while Nigel Martyn put in a virtuoso performance between the sticks. But it was Carsley who will be remembered.

Popping up on the edge of the box infront of the Gwladys Street, the ball pinged back to him and he instinctively shot around an advancing defender and past the hapless Chris Kirkland. The Street End went wild, and the resulting "piley-on" from the players became an iconic image for Evertonians, which Carsley on the bottom and Tim Cahill atop holding a thumb up to his manager on the touchlines.

90. James Vaughan's first Everton goal

Goodison Park was bathed in sunshine as the Toffees strolled past a relegation threatened Crystal Palace side. Everton dominated from start to finish with goals courtesy of Arteta, Cahill and a certain young phenomenon.

With ten minutes to spare and Everton three goals to the good, David Moyes took the opportunity to allow James Vaughan to become the youngest ever Everton player, surpassing Joe Royle's landmark by almost a fortnight. The records didn't end there.

As expected, Vaughan chased and harried and got the biggest reward of all with a few minutes left on the clock - a debut goal into the Gwladys Street end. A long throw from the ever reliable Nigel Martyn found Kilbane, who elected to surge past two Palace defenders in a frenzy of pace and power. A low left foot cross was met by the stretching teenager to make it 4-0, game over, and yet another record secured - this time becoming the Premiership's youngest ever goalscorer, and an unbelievable feeling of elation swept the stadium.

Goodison rocked, the pain of a Wayne Rooney's departure was drained away, we had found our new teenage idol, and his name was James Vaughan.

91. Duncan Ferguson's winner against Manchester United in 2005

The Blues were on fire in the 2004-05 season, and against all odds were flying high in the Premier League. The commentators all predicted that this game would separate the men from the boys, and that order would be restored and United would ride out winners. Everton proved them wrong, as they had so many times that season.

Tim Cahill showed the spirit the whole side had shown during the game when he was late out from half time due to a spell of vomiting after putting in so much effort in midfield, while Nigel Martyn showed why David Moyes had shown so much faith in him even at his advanced age.

After an hour, Mikel Arteta was awarded a free kick on the left of the pitch, and 30-something Duncan Ferguson was poised to make a £30m defender look distinctly average. Gaining six yards on Rio Ferdinand, Ferguson rose majestically to head Everton into a one goal lead to thunderous noise from the whole of Goodison Park. United were to have Paul Scholes and Gary Neville sent off later in the game as Everton battled to a fantastic 1-0 victory.

92. Every time Z-Cars is played

Z-Cars, the TV cop show of the 1960's, broke the mould in TV drama, and became an instant hit with TV audiences world-wide. Filmed in Kirkby, and with several of the cast members supporting the Blues, a visit to Goodison Park was marked by the playing of the theme tune as the teams ran out onto the pitch.

It was an instant success with the fans, and soon after was adopted on a permanent basis. The second the drums start up, you know the time has come for Everton to play, and it never fails to send the hairs on the back of every Evertonian's head stand on end.

> *Every time I hear Z-Cars it brings a tear to my eye....Evertonian Stephen Bellis*

93. Tim Cahill's celebrations as Everton finish fourth in 2005.

Everton went into the last home game of the 2004-05 season knowing that beating Newcastle would clinch fourth place and a chance to compete in the Champions League.

All season, Evertonians had endured chants of "Champions League, you're having a laugh" but this game was the chance to have the last laugh. And laugh we did.

David Weir headed the blues into the lead in the first half, and as Newcastle seemed content to just enjoy their day out, Tim Cahill smashed the blues into a 2-0 lead, and into Europe.

He wheeled away from goal with his determined and ecstatic run and signalled that it was all over, Everton would finish fourth, and that no-one could question our standing at the top of the English game.

94. Andrew Johnson's "3-0" celebration as the Blues beat Liverpool in September 2006

This was truly and magnificently one of the proudest moments of my life, tears came to my eyes, tears of true joy...Everton fan Darren Cleland

Andy Johnson had become Everton's record signing just a few months earlier and had got his goalscoring underway early on, and was in perfect form to face Liverpool on September 9th 2006.

Everton had not beaten Liverpool by three goals for thirty years, but when Johnson capitalised on poor defending to put Everton 2-0 up in the first half, Goodison Park knew something special was happening, although we had to wait until the last minute to send the Kopites home with the image of Andy Johnson holding up three fingers on one hand and a big fat zero on the other as he wheeled away into the Park End.

Liverpool keeper Reina fumbled Lee Carsley's long shot and as Johnson ran in, the Spaniard appeared to drop the ball onto his head for the England international to put the blues ahead. 3-0 was too much for most Liverpool fans and the away end emptied as if someone had pulled the plug out.

95. James McFadden's last minute wonder-goal against Charlton

A drab affair, Everton's fixture with Charlton in April 2007 was heading for a goal-less draw, with the highlight being Darren Bent's shot which ended up going out for a throw-in in his own half. Until the last 10 minutes when James McFadden decided to show us a rare glimpse of his genius.

The ball was scrambled clear to the edge of the Charlton box after Joleon Lescott had put Everton ahead, and Bent had equalised, and 'Faddy' shaped to shoot with his left foot. However, at the last moment he changed his mind, and the shot turned into a cheeky lob over the advancing defender before he completed his left foot volley after running behind his opponent to smash the ball into the net.

96. Turning Nuremberg Blue

When Everton were drawn away to Nuremburg in 2007's UEFA Cup group stages, no-one would have predicted the invasion that would follow as up to 15,000 Evertonians travelled to Germany in search of some European adventure. They weren't disappointed.

The city became a sea of Blue and White, and the locals welcomed their Evertonian visitors with open arms as the famous name of Everton and the reputation for good behaviour on tour went ahead of us.

The police posed for photos, the locals put on some wonderful hospitality, and Everton won the match. What more could you want from an Everton away day in Europe? Many Nuremburg fans posted on Everton website forums for days after the game stating how great it had been and hoping that next year's draw would put the two teams together again as once again Evertonians showed themselves as the best in the world.

97. The celebrations at the end of the 2006-07 season as Everton clinched another season in the UEFA Cup.

Two years earlier, our European adventure had ended in bitter disappointment, but when Everton qualified for the UEFA Cup at the end of the 2006-07 season, there was a sense of belief that this time would be different.

Portsmouth were the visitors on the final day of the season and as with Everton needing a win to end the visitors' own hopes of a European adventure, the Blues turned on the style. Mikel Arteta teamed up wonderfully in midfield with Manuel Fernandes and it wasn't long before shouts of "Ole" were heard from all quarters of Goodison Park as the Spaniard fired Everton ahead from the penalty spot.

"We're all going on a European tour" was the chant of choice as Joseph Yobo put the Blues 2-0 up, and even Gary Naysmith got in on the act by bagging a third just before the end in his last appearance for the Blues in the Premier League.

Players and fans celebrated after the match in the lap of honour and Evertonians knew that their next European adventure was on its way, and that it would be one to remember.

> Does it have to be only one? If it does then scoring the goal in the FA Cup semi-final in 1966 against Manchester United to get us to Wembley.
>
> But, if I'm allowed any more, then the night we beat West Brom to clinch the league title in 1970 at Goodison Park, which was a wonderful night. And then getting the cap for England comes a close third.
>
> They are the three moments I treasure from my career, I think in that order!
>
> **Colin Harvey** – Everton player, coach, manager.

98. Yakubu's celebration after scoring Everton's league first penalty of the season in the last game of the season in the 2007-08 season.

Everton were the only Premier League side not to be awarded a penalty in the Premiership in the 2007-08 season, until 9 minutes before the end of the season.

Leon Osman was fouled as he made a darting run into the Newcastle penalty area and referee Peter Walton pointed to the spot to give the Blues their first penalty of the season.

Yakubu stepped up and scored his 21st goal of the season, and Evertonians got to see the now trademark celebration as "the Yak" joined the party in the Park End as Everton clinched fifth place and UEFA Cup football for the following season.

99. Mikel Arteta's goal against Fiorentina at Goodison Park in the 2007-08 UEFA Cup

Everton's journey in the UEFA Cup in 2008 was going fantastically well, winning all of the group stage games after an unsteady start against Metalist Kharkiv in the Ukraine. Then came the real test in the Quarter Finals, against Italian side Fiorentina, and in the first leg, that test had proven to be too much for a tired Everton side, leaving the second leg at Goodison Park all set to be a classic Everton night.

The game sold out in record time, and with a capacity crowd inside the stadium on a cold, but dry, Thursday evening, Everton's players were expected to deliver. They did not disappoint during the 120 minutes.

Andy Johnson scored Everton's first off his hip, and the stadium erupted. Everton were back in the tie, and were dominating their opponents who were struck like rabbits in the headlights.

Fiorentina's keeper had the game of his life, saving from Yakubu and Osman before the break, but in the second half, no keeper would have saved what was to come.

Mikel Arteta picked up the ball just inside the Fiorentina half, near the Bullens Road stand, looked up, and started on a run towards the Gwladys Street goal. The Fiorentina defenders backed off, perhaps expecting the ball to be pushed out to the overlapping runner, but instead, Arteta, 25 yards from goal, unleashed a wicked shot that nestled beautifully in the far corner of the goal, and Goodison Park erupted once again in a crescendo of rapturous ecstasy.

100. Securing "The Everton Collection"

Brought together by Dr David France, "The Everton Collection" is the biggest single collection of football memorabilia in the world, and comprises 95% of programmes ever printed for an Everton match, as well as ledgers detailing every aspect of the club's early history – including many of the moments from this book.

Bought using a combination of lottery funding and money raised by Evertonians, this vast collection of priceless Everton history will be displayed for all Everton fans to see. From the first medal presented to an Everton player, to the minutes of the meeting which saw the split from Anfield owner John Houlding, every detail of Everton's history will be preserved for future generations.

My dad claimed that we were god's club and that the big Blue upstairs would send us one of his own to lead us from the post-war gloom.

As a kid, I had endured the efforts of Harris, Kirby, Llewellyn and Wignall before the arrival of my hero. Even though I had read about his role in breaking the Old Firm's grip on Scotland's silverware,

I was ill-prepared for the sheer beauty of his play. It was love at first sight. He didn't run, he glided across the turf. He didn't turn, he pirouetted. He didn't jump, he floated. He didn't kick the ball, he caressed it. In fact, his touch was like a mother's tender kiss. He possessed radar vision. And when required, his boots dispatched missiles. Above all, he had eye-catching grace and as long as Everton survives, men will talk in awe of his sublime skills.

Despite his super-sized blisters, hearing loss and on-going feud with his boss, he made us proud to be Blue. In fact my hero is second only to William Ralph

Dean in our folklore. Dixie's contributions can be measured by the number of times he hit the back of the net, whereas my hero's can be characterized by the number of times he took our breath away.

My favourite Everton memory was the title decider with Spurs on 20 April 1963. We dominated the game and had struck the woodwork on numerous occasions. Football memories are inherently idealised but I can close my eyes and picture him soaring two feet above the Tottenham defence to power the match winner past Bill Brown.

Gwladys Street erupted. It's the only time that I had seen grown men cry at a match. My dad was right, Alex Young is proof that not too long ago God was a Blue and wanted us to be happy.

David France

Football memorabilia? One man's trash is another man's rubbish. Well that's what I thought until my husband unearthed 'The Everton Scriptures'.

These are the 29 leather-bound volumes which trace how the initiatives of the enthusiastic amateurs of St Domingo grew into an EPL worldwide franchise. They chronicle the decisions made at the weekly and emergency meetings of the board of directors. In total there are 10,000 pages hand-written by John Houlding, George Mahon, Will Cuff and John Moores which document Everton's involvement in the founding of the Football League, the acrimonious departure from Anfield and subsequent birth of LFC, the construction of Goodison Park and the selection of team colours as well as all scouting appraisals, transfer negotiations and team selections. Incredibly, the first volume was discovered in a humble junk shop.

Given its neglected condition, it took me a while to understand what I was looking at. Nevertheless, I found it inconceivable that it had been discarded by the club. After I had skimmed the contents, my better half announced his plans to rescue any other similar volumes. And one by one they surfaced via a network of memorabilia dealers.

Some were more expensive than others. Irrespective of the funds involved and time expended, my favorite Everton memory is the acquisition which completed the unbroken run of 'The Everton Scriptures' dating from 1887 to 1964. This final and elusive volume cost more than hard cash. The transaction involved some of Dixie Dean's medals.

Of course we were only ever the guardian of these treasures albeit for a dozen or so years but to be honest I was relieved to see the back of them. In the end, we donated them to an independent public body, namely the Everton Charitable Trust, so that all Blues can access their rich history.

Elizabeth France

The 100 Greatest Everton Moments

Acknowledgements

To create a book such as this, and to create and maintain a website such as NSNO, a tremendous amount of assistance is required, and without the people who have provided that help, there would be no book, and no website.

The first person I have to thank is my partner Carla, who puts up with the continual invasions into our home and lives that Everton provide, and has helped mould and create NSNO.co.uk much more than she will ever allow me to give her credit for. She helped choose the people who moderate and write for the site; Chris, Andy, Joe, and Liam, without whom the site would often grind to a halt and the regular updates many have come to rely upon would not be made. Their contributions to the book have been great, and their continued work on NSNO is the lifeblood of the site.

Steve Milne and Martin O'Boyle have given life-changing advice and reminders at times, and their support of the site and myself has been an inspiration. Ian MacDonald, of the Independent Blues, has been an inspiration in his support of not only NSNO, but of Everton. I hope he finally writes a book of his experiences with the Blues, although it'll need a few volumes!

All the authors who have written textbooks that I have referred to here and that have provided fantastic reading throughout my Evertonian life. To those who continue to provide the fanzines we buy on matchdays, not least to George Orr and his wonderful "Blueblood" historical and contemporary fanzine (on sale outside the Winslow on matchdays!)

It would be remiss to not thank every player who has ever played for Everton, or any manager who has ever managed the club, who have provided us with these memorable moments – many more than this book explores – and those who I have shared them with. I've met some wonderful Blues over the years, and I hope to meet many more!

And finally, it wouldn't be right if I didn't end the book with my own "greatest Everton moment" would it? There have been hundreds to choose from but I think the first time I ever walked up the steps on the Gwladys Street and saw the lush green turf of Goodison open up infront of me. The massiveness of Goodison Park hitting you for the first time, combined with the unique smell that used to accompany football stadia before the smoking ban is enormous. A real life-defining moment, and the instant you realize that Everton is the club for you.

Simon Paul, 2008

Images

Accrington Stanley programme – provided with permission by Dr David France

Cover artwork – created by Simon Paul, cover photo taken by Simon Paul.

Floodlit derby ticket scan – provided with permission by Dr David France

"Goodison Park by night" – taken by Rhys Hicks and submitted for use by NSNO in our "Goodison Gallery"

Harvey, Kendall and Ball – photo courtesy of Ian MacDondald

"FA Cup Final programme 1984" – after three months trying to source the owner of the copyright of this image, we feel we have exhausted all reasonable avenues to try and give appropriate credit to the owner of this image. However, if you feel you own this copyright, then please contact us via the website and we will discuss the use of the image and further accreditation of copyright notices.

Rotterdam 1985 – submitted to NSNO by Colin Wilkes and used with written permission with thanks.

Medals – Image provided with permission by Dr David France

Bibliography

In no particular order...

Dr Everton's Magnificent Obsession *by David France*

One Hundred Years of Goodison Glory *by Ken Rogers*

Everton : The School of Science *by James Corbett*

The Blue Correspondent *by Billy Smith*

The Official Centenary History *by John Roberts*

Dixie Dean *by John Keith*

One Step Ahead *by Duncan McKenzie*

30 *by Bob Latchford and Martin O'Boyle*

25 Seasons at Goodison *The Complete Record*

Memories of Everton *by Kevin Ratcliffe*

Everton's FA Cup 100

Talking Blue *by Becky Tallentire*

Still Talking Blue *by Becky Tallentire*

The subscribers and supporters on the following pages have made this book possible, thank you to each and every one of you...

101. Simon Paul
102. Liam Thompson
103. Joe Jennings
104. Andy Baker
105. Chris Lee
106. Dave Prentice
107. Phil Thomas
108. David Boyle
109. Mark Evenden
110. Malte Christian Hestbech
111. Martin O'Boyle
112. Andy Weir
113. David Doran
114. Stephen Rogers
115. Stephen McIntyre
116. Chris March
117. Stuart Moore
118. Kenneth Wilson
119. Daniel Salewski
120. Francis Dadez
121. Mike Ode
122. Jim Weedon
123. Brian Collins
124. Paula Wilkinson
125. Joe Burgess
126. David Quinn
127. David Briscoe
128. Ann Ralph
129. Anthony Horabin
130. Darren Cleland
131. Julian Outram
132. Dennis Stevens
133. Steve Bellis
134. Stuart Forrester
135. John Pickersgill
136. Andrew Snee
137. Rob Westerberg
138. Thomas Lynch

139. John Kenny
140. Christina Connor
141. Matthew Bowen
142. Nigel Fletcher
143. Scott Walker
144. Paul Rodgers
145. Danny Dunn
146. Phil Thomas
147. Tom Gill
148. Steve Milne
149. Ian MacDonald
150. James Corbett
151. John McQuade
152. Becky Tallentire
153. Paul MacDonald
154. Paul Simpson
155. Steven Warburton
156. George Orr
157. Tony Kay
158. Derek Mountfield
159. Simon Fletcher
160. Marko Sagadin
161. Alex Young
162. Ray Wilson
163. David France
164. Mike Turner
165. Eryl Ann Elias

Printed in Poland
by Amazon Fulfillment
Poland Sp. z o.o., Wrocław